QUESTIONS ASKED AND ANSWERED
FROM THE FIELD

SIMPLY
INSTRUCTIONAL
COACHING

FOREWORD BY STEVE BARKLEY

NICOLE S. TURNER

Simply Instructional Coaching

Questions Asked and Answered from the Field

Written by Nicole S. Turner

Published by:
© 2019 Simply Coaching and Teaching, LLC

Simply Instructional Coaching
By Nicole S. Turner

Copyright © 2019 Nicole S. Turner.

Published by Simply Coaching and Teaching LLC

ISBN: 978-0-578-52740-6

Library of Congress Control Number: 2019907280

Editor: Melba Hopper
Interior Designer: Ashley Hughes
Cover Designer: Vampitrela

Printed in the United States of America

First printing edition 2019.

Simply Coaching and Teaching LLC
9801 Fall Creek Rd Ste. 150
Indianapolis, IN 46256

www.simplycoachingandteaching.com

Dedication

In loving memory of my father, Perry T. Turner, Sr. Although you are no longer physically present in my life, I still feel your impact every day. Thank you for instilling in me that anything is possible with faith, hard work, and determination.

In loving memory of my big brother, Monte G. Johnson Jr., Thank you for all of the wonderful memories of growing up and your words of wisdom they have stayed close in my heart and given me hope when I had nothing to pull on.

To my mom, Helen. It's impossible to thank you adequately for everything you've done, from loving me unconditionally to raising me to have values and to celebrate and embrace life. Thank you for pouring yourself into me; I could never understand a mother's love until now.

To my oldest son, Josh. Having you was one of the best decisions in my life. As your mother, it is my job to teach you about life, but you have taught me what life is all about. When God blessed me with you, my life changed, and it was one of the greatest days of my life.

To my one and only daughter, Kristyn. You are one of the most beautiful miracles in my life and one of the greatest joys I know. You are the true meaning of persistence and determination. You may have outgrown my lap, but you will never outgrow my heart.

To my youngest son, Maurice Justin. You are so smart, funny, and full of life. You have made this family complete. You have helped to create some of the happiest memories of the past, the most joyous moments of the present, and the hope and promise of the future.

To my best friend, Rick. Thank you for believing in me when I was too weak and exhausted to believe in myself; for always knowing who I am and reminding me of that when I forgot; for pushing me beyond all measures, not judging me when I did something really, really crazy; and for always being honest. I have no doubt that you are genuinely concerned with the outcome of my life and my children. Thank you for doing all the things a real best friend does. I could never repay you for being you.

Last but not least, to all of the wonderfully dedicated teachers and instructional coaches in this world who have made a commitment to being a special part of children's lives forever, continue the work, this is for you!

Table of Contents

Foreword

Simply Instructional Coaching

I benefited from instructional and peer coaching before I had heard the terms. My teacher preparation program and my initial teaching roles were built around team models that had formal and informal coaching conversations built into the organizational structure. When I first began consulting with teachers in other schools, I was surprised to find working in isolation to be the common practice. More puzzling was teachers' belief that the breaking of that isolation was an infringement rather than a gift. In 1982 Bruce Joyce and Beverly Showers wrote "The Coaching of Teachers" (https://www.ascd.org/ASCD/pdf/journals/ed_lead/el_198210_joyce.pdf), which included a comparison of coaching athletes with coaching teachers. This statement reinforced my view that we all deserve a coach:

> "Perhaps the most striking difference in training athletes and teachers is their initial assumptions. Athletes do not believe that mastery will be achieved quickly or easily. They understand that enormous effort results in small increments of change. We on the other hand have often behaved as though teaching skills were so easily acquired that a simple presentation, one-day workshop, or single-videotaped demonstration were sufficient to ensure successful classroom performance. To the extent that we have communicated this message to teachers we have probably misled them. Learning to use an inductive strategy for the learning of concepts is probably at least as difficult as learning to throw a block properly."

At times the phrase "everyone needs a coach" has been used to communicate to teachers why they should engage in coaching with an instructional coach or peer. I have found I am able to generate a more exploratory conversation with the approach that everyone deserves a coach. How do you communicate that coaching is a gift that teachers deserve?

In *Simply Instructional Coaching*, Nicole has built answers too many questions that instructional coaches have raised with her as they accepted, and in many cases built, their roles in schools. Parts I and II examine questions concerning the definitions of coaching and the roles that instructional coaches can play. It's critical that clarity in roles be reached so that a partnership with administrators and trust with teachers can be built.

Coaches need to consciously implement verbal communication skills that are built around effective listening, questioning, and paraphrasing. Questions such as _How do I help teachers set goals?_ and _How does being data-driven fit into my role as a coach and my coaching cycle?_ are addressed in the skills and strategies sections of Parts III and IV.

Coaches are often called upon to provide both formal and informal professional development as well as support for existing or newly forming Professional Learning Communities. These are critical activities as they provide an opportunity for the coach to "model the model." How are the practices that engage students in rigorous inquiry modeled in PD activities? How does a coach show her vulnerability and risk-taking as a participant in PLCs, modeling the actions that are desired of students in classrooms and teachers in collaborative problem-solving. Questions around professional development and PLCs are addressed in Part V of this text.

As a coach you will find teachers may approach the "need to change" being:

- Unaware (They think they are already achieving the desired student outcomes)
- Getting Ready (They know they need to change, but not yet)
- Started (In the learning dip as they start to change)
- Developing (They are seeing the payoffs of the change being implemented)
- Unwilling (No attempts or plans to change)

In the last section, questions concerning relationships with teachers in various mindsets and stages are addressed.

I believe that an exciting reason to be an educator is that there is no mountaintop to our career. As I have now passed year forty of my career, I'm amazed at all there is to learn about teaching and learning. As an instructional coach, you are in a great position to continue your learning while guiding others to do the same. What are the strategies you will use to build a continuous improvement culture? What opportunities do you provide for the best to grow? How do you model your personal continuous development?

As you begin, Nicole has provided lots of questions and answers to ponder. It's your turn to Simply Instructional Coach.

Best wishes on this very important work!

Steve Barkley

Steve Barkley is the executive vice-president of PLS3rdLearning and the author of _Instructional Coaching with the End in Mind_ and _Quality Teaching in a Culture of Coaching_. His weekly blogs and podcasts for school leaders at all levels can be found at www.barkleyPD.com.

Congratulations on your Coaching Position!

Are you ready to get in there and be the best instructional coach you can be?

Absolutely you are! That is why you purchased this book. However, first let me say: This is not a typical instructional coaching book focused on research and theory; I don't discuss instructional strategies and classroom management strategies that you can offer teachers that will help them in the classroom; and I don't go into deep details on research about teachers' thought patterns. You can find all those wonderful things in other coaching books. Yes, I think those books and that information are essential to being an instructional coach. However, as a coach of coaches, I know that so many things get lost when you are transitioning into the position. One day you are hired and the next thing you know, it's the first day of school and you have no idea what you are doing, how your leader envisions your position, how to approach a teacher as a coach, and what a coaching cycle is. You don't even know how you fit into the scheme of things, because you are not an administrator or a classroom teacher; you are somewhere in the middle, straddling the fence, trying to find your place in the system. I have been there, and it took some time to figure it all out, which is why I created this book.

Simply Instructional Coaching will help you create a plan and think through your next steps as you assume the role of a coach. It provides the "how-to" cliff notes on getting started as an instructional coach. *This book* includes answers to many questions that new and seasoned coaches have asked time and again that you can reflect on. The final goal is that you will then be able to implement simple instructional coaching processes that will have the greatest impact on your coaching efforts and, in turn, the greatest impact on teacher learning and student achievement.

It's time to get started!

Happy Coaching,

Nicole

Introduction

"Instructional coaching should be *impactful* not *overwhelming*."
—*Nicole S. Turner*

When I became a teacher, I never sought to be an instructional coach. Truth be told, I never knew the position even existed. But I remember the day I fell in love with helping teachers. It was my fourth year of teaching, and each year I had been moved from school to school and position to position. There was a surplus of teachers, and I was what they called a "RIF" (reduction in force) teacher each year. This particular year was no different from the other years, except I was in my principal preparation program and had to do my "internship" hours outside the classroom. I began the school year in the high school in my district. Even though my license was for K–6, I took the position temporarily, and it worked out great. I got a chance to get high school experience from the classroom perspective and work with one of the high school vice-principals. For those three months, I learned a ton, and finally understood what leadership was all about.

One of my internship assignments was to work one-on-one with a teacher to improve instruction. My mentor principal paired me with a teacher who was struggling with creating strong lessons in the classroom. I doubted myself because it was high school and I knew that high school teachers were very strong in content knowledge. How would I help a high school teacher? I was a strong teacher, but my background was on the elementary school level. My elementary knowledge on developing lessons for all content helped me to guide this teacher in the right direction. I used my knowledge of instructional strategies, and the teacher's lessons turned around. We met on Tuesdays and Thursdays for two hours after school. We worked on lesson plans and on practicing and talking through how the lesson would be delivered. The feeling of helping a teacher improve also helped me identify the type of leader I wanted to be. I wanted not only to lead a school to success but also to help teachers in classrooms be better teachers and improve their delivery of instruction, which would ultimately benefit their students.

As my career went on and I began to gain leadership experience, I was hired as a differentiated accountability coach for the district I was working for. It was a great opportunity, but I didn't know exactly what I was doing. I was trying everything out. I hosted weekly data meetings and entered data into spreadsheets, discussed lesson plans and the implementation of them, met with the principal and covered lunch duty. I was trying my best, and although we saw some gains in instruction, I can't say 100 percent that they came from my coaching. But that year, I learned how to be an instructional coach. I leaned on books about coaching, talked with other coaches, and even got myself a coach and started creating and developing a system for coaching. After five years in different roles from assistant principal, instructional coach, and even school improvement specialist at the Indiana Department of Education, I had developed systems and procedures to ensure that my coaching can make an impact. Simply Instructional Coaching is my way of sharing my years of experience with you.

In Part I, you will read about what constitutes the position of an instructional coach. You will also discover that there are many different instructional coaching models and roles a coach can play in schools and districts. Moreover, because often as teachers and coaches, we put others before ourselves and don't take care of ourselves. So, I will share with you a few things that I do to ensure that I keep the coach—life balance.

In Part II, you will find information on transitioning into an instructional coaching role. Whether you are a new or seasoned coach, you will find some takeaways. I share my top best practices, top coaching mistakes and how to avoid them, how to be reflective, time-management and scheduling strategies, how to be organized, and how to create a coaching philosophy.

In Part III, I share the best practices I use to support teachers in the classroom. I delve into ways to create an environment that provides balanced support for teachers and how to give meaningful feedback and constructive criticism, as well as how to set goals with teachers, how to develop coaching plans, how to utilize communication strategies, how to establish top coaching strategies when working with teachers, and the "musts" needed for beginning a successful year.

In Part IV, I identify what an instructional coaching cycle is and define its purpose, how to utilize a coaching cycle that will benefit teachers and students, how to increase effectiveness, how to coach conversations, and how to use data as a coach.

In Part V, I discuss PLCs, team planning meetings, and the essential task of an instructional coach, delivering professional development sessions. The "how-to" is included to create and deliver an effective professional development session.

In Part VI, last but not least, I discuss building relationships and trust with your teachers. This is the staple of your work as an instructional coach. I discuss working with adults, fixed mindsets, and resistant teachers; dealing with conflict on a team; and even some strategies for building a strong relationship with your principal.

I answer each question with suggestions and provide some step-by-step processes that can make the suggestions easy to implement. In addition, after each question, you will find a coaching thought and a reflection thought that can jumpstart your own reflections and prompt you to write about your immediate next steps. As you reflect on your role as an instructional coach, realize that you will be implementing change and that change requires courage and consistency—the courage to step out of your comfort zone of being a classroom teacher and to approach, celebrate, coach, and lead others to success; the consistency needed to implement coaching cycles again and again until you see change happening. Don't give up. You will have hard days, sad days, happy days, and lonely days. Never forget why you started and never forget that, at heart, you and I were and always will be teachers who do what is in the best interest of children.

Part I

The Hype Around Instructional Coaching

"Coaching is the universal language of change and learning"
- CNN

"Instructional coaching is fundamentally about teachers, teacher leaders, school administrators and central office leaders examining practice in reflective ways with a strong focus on student learning and results as the ultimate barometer of improvement"
- Annenberg Institute for School Reform

What is an instructional coach?

At the core, an instructional coach is someone whose role is to work with teachers and school leaders to improve the educational outcomes of their students.

The instructional coach is the center of the instructional coaching model. The coach is put in place to deliver high-quality professional development in several ways. Teachers are supported by instructional coaches in areas such as content, instruction, organization, and management.

The instructional coaching system comes to life when the instructional coach partners closely with the school administration. The result? A powerhouse team responsible for high-quality instruction using co-planning, modeling, and feedback (just to name a few) to make sure it all happens.

As an instructional coach, you're not necessarily an expert in a certain subject. Your expertise lies in supporting teachers from any subject area.

Yet, instructional coaches can be assigned to a specific content area. For example, there are math coaches, ELA coaches, curriculum coaches, science coaches, social studies coaches, technology coaches, and academic coaches just to name a few. All of these content-specific coaches use the same coaching strategies to build teachers' effectiveness in the classroom.

Instructional coaches work toward clearly defined goals. Some examples might be:

- Increasing graduation rates
- Supporting teachers as they implement the latest state standards or the newest resources
- Encouraging equitable student participation to be disaggregated by ethnicity, gender, and socioeconomic status in all programs and student discipline data

Coaching Thought

When a strong infrastructure is dedicated to supporting teachers as they deepen and implement instructional practices, student achievement grows by leaps and bounds.

Now knowing the definition of an instructional coach, rewrite the definition in your own words thinking of yourself as the coach. Begin your definition with "I (insert your name) as your instructional coach will. . . ."

_____

_____

_____

_____

_____

_____

_____

_____

_____

_____

_____

_____

_____

What the instructional coaching model?

The instructional coaching model can be seen as a professional development model. Many disciplines use the term professional development. Doctors, educators, accountants, nurses, and even manufacturers all participate in professional development. According to BussinessDictionary.com, professional development is a "process of improving and increasing capabilities of staff through access to education and training opportunities in the workplace, through an outside organization, or through watching others perform on the job."

For many years, teachers have attended professional development (PD) sessions and seminars. The problem with PD is that research shows it to be ineffective without follow-up. After a teacher attends a professional development session, one of three things happens. One, the teacher says the PD was boring and leaves not knowing or understanding the approach or strategy taught and discussed. Therefore, the teacher never implements it in the classroom. Two, the teacher leaves the PD excited to try something new in the classroom. He/She plans and implements the new approach, and it doesn't go well; then the teacher struggles to adapt the strategy to his/her classroom but hits a brick wall and just gives up. Three, the teacher implements the strategy and it goes well, but the results are slow. This is what we call "train and hope." Teachers are "trained" on the new strategy or approach, and the administration "hopes" that it will work. But, as noted, in each of these situations, the strategy was not used or continued, and therefore the teachers' time and the money spent on the consultant were wasted. There was little to no evidence of change from implementing the strategy or approach.

Over time, it was realized that there was a need for ongoing support to implement strategies and approaches, and now we have the instructional coach model.

The purpose of the instructional coaching model is to help close the student achievement gap and accelerate learning for all students by building teacher capacity through the implementation of effective instructional practices (Casey, 2008). In other words, it allows for teachers to be "trained" on the new strategy or approach and to be supported through the implementation.

Coaching Thought

The instructional coach is the center of this model. The coach is the job-embedded professional learning for the classroom teacher. From your work as an instructional coach, there should be evidence of improvement in classroom management, instruction, and overall student learning.

Knowing you are the center of the coaching model, how will you measure your work? Jot down a few ways you want to measure your work at the end of the school year. Example: My second year of coaching, I decided I wanted to see how my communication with teachers improved over the year. So I created a beginning of the year, a middle of the year, and an end of the year survey for the teachers I supported to complete and for me to review. I made sure that they were anonymous (I used SurveyMonkey) and asked for honest feedback. This helped to shape my work, and I was able to see my growth based on the answers. I asked the exact same questions each time just in a different order.

_____
_____
_____
_____
_____
_____
_____
_____
_____
_____
_____
_____
_____
_____

What the different coaching focus models?

Research has shown that coaching works. Helping teachers to get through the rough spots while in the classroom benefits not only the teacher but also the students and the field of education itself. With the alarming rate of teachers leaving the field of education to do other things, many students are now lacking teachers who are experienced in their craft. Coaching is one way to help retain teachers in the field. As a result, several coaching models have surfaced. I am sharing the three models that I have used in my work as a coach and that I use in my work as I coach other coaches.

Student-Centered: Student-centered coaching is based generally on student learning and outcomes. The teacher and coach watch data and assessments to determine whether the methods they have employed are successful. There is less focus on the coach–teacher relationship and more of a shared goal of increasing the percentage of students meeting standards. Assessments are used to determine progress and achievement of students toward meeting goals, and that data is analyzed by the teacher and coach together to determine future goals and instructional methods. When I started using the model, I referenced several of Diane Sweeney's books on Student-Centered Coaching. I normally use this model when I am working with a more experienced teacher.

Teacher-Centered: Teacher-Centered coaching, as it sounds, focuses on the teacher and what can be done to improve instruction. Beginning with assessing current student progress, the coach guides the teacher in using evidence-based strategies with technology and curriculum as tools to move forward. In this model, the coach holds teachers accountable in making progress. Assessments are done for this purpose as well, and the focus is on how to improve the teachers' methods and outcomes. A lot of weight is given to the teachers' ability to self-analyze and reflect on the "why" behind their lessons, educational choices, and beliefs. I use this model mostly when I am coaching new and struggling teachers. The goal is teacher improvement.

Relationship-Driven: Relationship-driven coaching focuses on the relationship between teacher and instructional coach. In this model, teacher and coach are viewed as equals, and there is not a spotlight on accountability. The teacher is able to make independent choices for the classroom. There is little focus on data. The coach is more of a support person for the teacher, providing resources and collaboration. Both the teacher and the coach take the position of learners. The coach might help facilitate reflection and self-analysis of methods, but not in a demanding or threatening manner. I use this method with teachers who are very experienced and need support in the curriculum or rigorous areas versus those who need help with classroom culture and management and how to teach a specific strategy.

Coaching Thought

As a coach, you must learn to be flexible and meet the needs of the teacher. Learning how to implement each of these models all at the same time is crucial to your work.

Adapted from : https://dianesweeney.com/wp-content/uploads/2015/05/Handouts-for-General-Session.pdf

How can you become more proficient in these models? What will you need to do next?

_____

_____

_____

_____

_____

_____

_____

_____

_____

_____

_____

_____

_____

_____

_____

_____

_____

What the different roles of an instructional coach?

Everyone you meet is, of course, familiar with the role of a teacher or a principal. But what's your unique role as an instructional coach?

As an instructional coach, you must be ready to wear many different hats.

Your main role is to utilize research-based best practices in your work with classroom teachers. You will encourage teacher growth through modeling, reflection, data analysis, and high-quality professional development, and this comes in many different forms.

Let's take a look at a few roles that you may encounter as an instructional coach:

> Supporter of student learning: As the "supporter of student learning," you may design and sometimes co-teach instruction to specifically focus on the diverse needs of students, setting standards-based goals, co-planning/co-teaching, developing differentiated instruction, designing formative assessments or assessments for learning, and creating strategies for standards-based grading. Meanwhile, you'll be diving into a collaborative analysis of student work and performance data.

> Supporter of effective instruction: As the "supporter of effective instruction," you will support the implementation of effective instructional strategies. You'll model instruction to give teachers a front-row look at effective practices. You'll also co-plan with a focus on developing a robust repertoire of pedagogical practices. During coaching cycles, as an instructional coach, you'll observe instruction as well as provide specific feedback. In some cases, you'll build teacher capacity by working with intervention groups for short periods of time.

Curriculum and content facilitator: As the "curriculum or content facilitator," you will step into this role by implementing either the Common Core Standards or the state adopted standards through adopted curricula. To make this happen, you'll work with teachers to unpack the standards and create learning targets while increasing teacher content knowledge. As a coach, you'll facilitate a better understanding of the structure of the written, taught, and tested curriculum. Dissecting standards to guide identification of essential knowledge and skills is a key part of this role.

Data coach: As the "data coach," you will lead conversations around data. When putting on the hat of data coach, get ready to facilitate conversations using data to drive instructional decisions. You might find yourself collaborating with teachers to analyze formative and summative student achievement data and assisting teachers with the use of data to improve student learning.

Facilitator for change/change agent: As the "facilitator for change/ change agent," you'll engage teachers in reflective thinking while they look at their own instructional practices critically and analytically. You'll rise to the challenge of providing a safe, trusting environment for teachers as you introduce alternatives and refinements for instructional practices.

Learner: As the "learner," you'll be called on to engage in continuous learning; a large part of your job is to keep current when it comes to professional development opportunities and professional reading. "Learner" was the original role for every professional in the field of education. The instructional coach is no exception.

Professional learning facilitator: As the "professional learning facilitator," you will design and facilitate useful professional learning opportunities for teachers and support staff. You'll be providing and facilitating all forms of professional development, whether it's teacher-led, district-led, or some other format. The goal is to bring forth the best practices for teachers to implement in the classroom. Your professional learning sessions should include activities and takeaways for teachers to implement right away.

Resource provider: As the "resource provider," you'll identify materials to enhance classroom instruction and student achievement. When teachers request it, you'll step in and identify instructional and assessment resources. You'll also share research and instructional best practices.

Coaching Thought

The practice of having you serve in multiple roles as an instructional coach within a school can create conflicts. For instance, it can be difficult for you to fulfill administrative duties—you may worry that your role as a peer to teachers is at risk. Teachers should never feel they are being evaluated by someone who is also serving as their coach! To prevent this dynamic, administrators need to clearly outline your coach role for everyone involved.

Now that you know the different roles an instructional coach can play, think about your roles in your building. What role will you perform the most, and what role you will perform the least? List these coaching roles from 1 to 8, with 1 being your most active role.

_____

_____

_____

_____

_____

_____

_____

_____

_____

_____

_____

_____

_____

_____

Coaches have told me that it is a stressful position. How can I take care of myself as an instructional coach?

Teachers in your building may think that you don't need to worry about self-care, because you have such a flexible schedule. You don't have to worry about grading essays over the weekend, and you typically don't get parent emails late at night. However, you will find that you quickly feel run-down if you don't take care of yourself the way you did as a classroom teacher. You may not have a set lunch time anymore, but that can sometimes mean that you skip lunch. You've traded your grading for some professional development book studies that you need to design or PowerPoint presentations for an in-service day that need to be created. If you're an interventionist for tiered students, you will most definitely still receive parent emails.

Here is a list of ten coping mechanisms to keep you mentally healthy.

Tip # 1 Take care of you: It's so important for you to take care of your whole self all the time but especially when you are in a high-stress situation. One way to take care of yourself is by exercising, whether that be running or going on a brisk walk around the track, gym, or hallway if you can't get away from work. If you can get away from work, yoga is a wonderful way to center yourself while gaining physical balance and working your tense muscles.

Tip #2 Watch what goes in: Another way to take care of yourself is monitoring what you ingest during the day. Keep in mind your body needs to stay hydrated to keep moving so a straight coffee and Diet Coke diet will not suffice. Drink plenty of water and keep healthy snacks with you to munch on throughout the day if needed. Also make sure you eat a well-balanced diet at home.

Tip #3 Talk it out: One of the best ways to destress is to talk out what you are stressed about (while remaining confidential). This is also a great opportunity to reconnect with friends and family. It's no secret that once school starts, our lives get busier (and if you have school-aged kids, they get busier). So take the time to call your best friend or your mom and just chat. You can use this time to get some stuff off your chest, or you can use it to not think about work at all.

Tip #4 Think calming thoughts: A great way to decompress is to allow yourself to go into a place of pure Zen. One way to get there is by getting a massage. A massage helps pull out bad energy and leaves you feeling so relaxed. Typically, after a massage, you get the best sleep of your life, so it helps in that department too. Another way to calm your mind is to light a candle and make true use of essential oils. Whether you diffuse them while you take a nice candle-lit bath or just use them as aromatherapy, they can be very helpful.

Tip #5 Be inspired: While you are taking that luxurious bubble bath, turn on an inspirational podcast to help motivate you. One of the most popular podcasters right now is Lewis Howes, who will be releasing a new book soon. He is currently doing three podcasts a week, and they will teach you how to be great; his focus is "a real-world guide to living your dreams, making an impact, and leaving a lasting legacy." Another great podcast to listen to is Gretchen Rubin's. Her newest show entitled Happier with Gretchen Rubin is co-hosted with her sister. It's taking the podcast world by storm and is there to help you "increase your happiness in life." These are just a few of the great podcasts you can listen to whether you are relaxing in the bath or on your way to work.

Tip #6 Make the great escape: Sometimes, what you really need is time for yourself. While you may be reading this thinking it sounds rather selfish, get that idea out of your mind. A little time just with "me, myself, and I" can be very therapeutic. Take in a funny movie or a comedy show. It's good for you to get out and get a laugh!

Tip #7 Change it up: Along with going on a hot date to the movies, you can take yourself out on a hot day to a salon. Whether that means dropping a little cash to get a new hairdo while you vent to your hairdresser or leaning back and getting a pedicure, taking care of yourself in this way is incredibly important too. We all know self-esteem is a big part of life, and sometimes what we need is a little pick-me-up and maybe a new pair of shoes to help us forget our work woes.

Tip #8 Read it: Getting lost in a book can be a great way to destress and focus your mind elsewhere. You can either read a book simply for pleasure (hello Nicholas Sparks) or you can focus on a self-help type book. A great book to look into is entitled *Practicing Mindfulness*. This book teaches you how to meditate correctly and discusses how science has shown the ways meditation can help you physically, mentally, and emotionally. Learning this art can come in handy in a variety of stressful situations.

Tip #9 Write it: If you're not the type of person to talk out your feelings, you can always choose to write about them. It's important to somehow let go of the stress you may be feeling, and if you're not a vocal person, writing is a great way to do it. Keeping a journal that talks about your thoughts and feelings is a great way to let things go, and it gives you something to reflect on later.

Tip #10 Just say . . . "NO": This is the best two-letter word in the entire dictionary, and as people in the field of education, we simply do not say it enough. Recognize what you can take on, and don't put too much on your plate. If you can't handle anymore at the moment, tell the person making the request that you simply don't have time. Learning how to say "no" when you need to will make your life so much less stressful in both the short term and the long term.

Stress is all around us every day and that's okay. Stress can be healthy when it's managed appropriately. Follow the preceding tips to help you be the best instructional coach you can be. Remember to take care of you. If you aren't at your best, will they be at theirs?

Check out https://www.healthline.com/health/stress/effects-on-body#3 for more tips.

Coaching Thought

The role of an instructional coach is stressful and lonely at times. Add to that being a mom/dad, husband/wife, aunt/uncle, daughter/son, and friend, and you are on overload. You need to know that it is important to take some time away for yourself. You must recognize that you are less able to handle the stresses of being a coach and life in general when you are depleted emotionally and physically exhausted. Do not feel guilty about taking a personal day. It's better to refresh yourself than to give only half of yourself. If you don't take time to rejuvenate, you will suffer, teachers will suffer, and students will suffer.

Think about what you did as a classroom teacher to implement self-care into your routine. Did you have a morning ritual that set you up for a happy morning? Did you make time to exercise before or after school? Did you dim the lights in your room and play calming music at certain times of the day? Identify three things you will do when times get tough. Write out how you will implement your self-care.

_____

_____

_____

_____

_____

_____

_____

_____

_____

_____

_____

_____

_____

Part II

Transitioning to the Instructional Coaching Role

"The most valuable resource that all teachers have is each other, without collaboration, our growth is limited by our own perspectives."

- Robert John Meehan

I just got my first instructional coaching role. What do I do? How do I transition?

Becoming a coach for the first time means you are super excited about what the year will hold for you, but you are also filled to the brim with nerves because communicating with adults instead of kids is a totally different ball game! Trust me, what you're feeling is normal.

If you were hired as an instructional coach, something about you as an educator stood out and helped you rise to the challenge. Focus on those strengths as you transition, because there will be many, many new things that may leave you feeling insecure if you don't keep what is so special about you near the front of your mind.

As you begin your school year, approach every new situation and coworker as a listener. You'll want to get to know your teachers and have a strong sense of their attitudes toward teaching. This all comes from listening more than talking. Do not stress too much about establishing yourself as being knowledgeable in certain areas of teaching. Everyone is assuming you know a little something about teaching—you were just hired to coach them! They will appreciate and trust you more in the long run if you take the time to engage them in conversations about their students and subject area(s) and really listen, rather than insert too much in areas in which you are not yet fully informed.

Being a listener helps you build trust and relationships with teachers and should be the anchor in every coaching relationship. Whether you are new to the building or are a tenured teacher making the transition to being a coach, you must build trust and relationships. If you worked with these teachers as a peer the previous year, they will be seeing you in a new light when you return from summer break as their instructional coach. Things may feel a little awkward for you and them as you all try to navigate how to interact with each other and the teachers determine whether they can have the same kind of rapport with you that they did when you were "one of them."

Thus, when transitioning to being an instructional coach, you first must focus on building trust and relationships, because they will open the doors to achieving any goals that you and your administration set for the school year. You cannot improve the use of data or implement PLCs in your building if the teachers do not see you as trustworthy and a member of their team. It is important to note that establishing yourself as a trusted teammate is not automatic or passive work. It takes intentionality and time to foster the kind of rapport you need to promote real change and growth. Do not make the mistake of waiting for teachers to recognize what a valuable resource you are; you must show them.

I coach many instructional coaches one-on-one, and one named Kate was an instructional coach at a school that was just opening. Her principal believed that her only responsibility for the entire first year was to build relationships (I totally agree), allowing time for everyone to get to know each other. The time for hard-hitting data analysis or strict instructional evaluation would begin in year two. Kate took this to mean that she should stay in the background, waiting for the teachers to come to her so that she didn't threaten or upset anyone. She spent her time ordering books for the school's leveled library and serving more as an administrative assistant to the principal through all of the chaos of opening a new building. She rarely met with teachers and ended that year feeling like she had done her job of not threatening any of the teachers or making them feel like she was there to evaluate them.

However, the issues arose in year two. The principal had big goals for the way teachers were going to do data chats and take pre- and post-test data to share with their teams during planning meetings. Kate got right to work scheduling time in her calendar to show up at each grade-level planning meeting to facilitate the discussions.

She was baffled when teachers were less-than-inviting when she asked to see their data and offered teaching strategies that might help improve student achievement. She was confused and struggled to understand why the teachers didn't see the good ideas she was bringing to the conversation. The problem was that they didn't know her well enough to trust her ideas! She had taken the idea of building trust and relationships as being one of staying in the background and not stepping on toes.

Coaching Thought

Building relationships with teachers is showing up and being a good listener, helping teachers to navigate the unknown waters of the curriculum, and even helping teachers identify their strengths and weaknesses. It's not serving in the background. While there is a time and place for such behavior, it's not at the beginning of your coaching journey. Being in the background did not serve Kate well in the long run. As a coach, you must let everyone know why you are there and what you can offer.

What is your biggest takeaway from Kate's experience? Write a few ideas on how you plan to transition into your role.

What are the top instructional coaching best practices?

You can grab a ton of different books on best practices for classroom instruction and management. You can find a few books on coaching practices as well. With any best practice, it is important to know that you must adapt those practices to your environment and culture. Each teacher, school building, district, and school principal are different, and how procedures are implemented in one building, classroom, or teacher doesn't mean it will work the same in another situation or building. Coaching practices should be differentiated for each teacher. You want to acquaint yourself with the best practices of coaching so that you can serve as a successful coach for your staff.

Here are a few best practices that have worked for me:

Make yourself visible: Greet people in the hallways, ask for some time to speak and share at different staff meetings. Create a monthly newsletter to tack onto your principal's email to teachers, or ask if you can send one out separately with professional development resources. Make a point to be seen and for teachers to know that you are not there to evaluate them, but to support student growth.

Make yourself available: In this book, you will read about setting up a schedule and managing your time well, but when teachers are in need, especially if they are asking for your help, you need to find a way to make yourself available to them. Although you want to protect your time, the truth is that your schedule is much more flexible than that of classroom teachers, so sometimes you need to make yourself fit into the structure of their day so as not to add extra stress to their plate.

Recognize that we all have differences and approach instruction differently . . . and stay positive about it: There may be times when the way you would do something is not at all the way a teacher is approaching it, and you feel the need to "fix it" by showing the teacher a totally different way of doing things that the teacher is not comfortable with. This can result in the teacher feeling overwhelmed, criticized, and less likely to ask you for help again.

My motto is, "If it's not broke, don't fix it." If what the teacher is doing is working just fine with students, there is no need to suggest or ask the teacher to do things differently. We are looking for results! Not a copycat of your classroom. To help teachers grow, smile, embrace your differences, and build on what they already know.

Maintain confidentiality: Establish trust with the teachers that you serve. A large part of establishing trust with teachers is conveying that you have their best interest in mind. The biggest thing I have learned is to be completely confidential. When you have your beginning-of-the-year conversation with your administrator, make it very clear that you are there to help teachers and students and that you are not there to be an evaluator or a spy. Setting this expectation with administrators helps them understand your commitment to your relationships with the teachers. You cannot be afraid to tell your administrator that you will keep some things confidential, and ask for that professional respect. Let your administrator know that you will share the things you are working on but may not go into great detail about the coaching conversations unless you deem it will hurt the staff or students in which you are serving.

Keep your word: When I was a little girl, my father and grandfather always told me that the only thing you have in this world was your word. Meaning that if you say you are going to do it, then do it! When you are building relationships with teachers all you have is your word. Especially if you are new to a building, many of the teachers don't know your work ethic or what you did in your previous roles. So in order for them to trust you, they need to know what they can expect from you and whether you are consistent. When keeping your word, make sure that you hold your commitments sacred and that you don't make promises you can't keep.

Communicate: Communication with teachers must be honest, open, and direct. You want to create a situation in which you and teachers can have healthy conversations. Set a tone that indicates your communication will be open, supportive, deliberate, and intentional. Your goal in communicating is to ensure that you can refocus teachers on their goals and give them what they need to be successful.

In doing so, be aware of your choice of words when you write emails and the tone of your voice when you speak. These are important factors because when teachers listen to you and read your words, they internalize the underlying message, which can make them feel good and supported or feel bad and attacked.

Listen: Listening is a skill that we as adults sometimes overlook. You must be intentional in listening to a teacher's goal with the intent to empathize and provide helpful feedback that impacts student learning. How many times have you been listening to a person and in your mind you are preparing your response before the person even stops talking? I know I have done this often, and so have my children and students. Before you respond to teachers, ensure that you really heard what they were trying to say and to validate their comments or concerns, repeat what they just said.

Reflect: Let's be real. No one is perfect, and all of us can use some improvements. So it is important to recognize that you can become better at what you do. In your instructional coaching schedule include time to reflect on your coaching week. Think about coaching conversations you had, teacher strategies you used and discussed, modeling that you implemented, and emails that you wrote. Document what went well and what didn't go so well, and determine next steps based on your discovery.

Manage: Frequently when we think of the word "management," we first think of managing people. But in our role, we have to manage time, tasks, consistency, and mood. Organization is key. Manage your time and schedule in a way that is realistic and effective. Review any tasks you have (planning meetings, teacher conversations, emails, professional development, testing schedules, etc.) and set priorities. Create a plan and schedule, and be consistent in implementing your routine. I must admit the one thing that is hard for me: it's exhibiting a productive and consistent mood during the day regardless of whether things are going well or not. I love what I do, but when I have a lot of things going on at once, I tend to shut down and get in grind mode. I am not happy and smiling, and when I am interrupted during my grind mode time, I can be a little bit agitated. So I have to stop in my tracks and manage my mood and remember that that I am a helper and can be interrupted.

Support teachers: Our goal is to improve student learning. We can best do so by supporting teachers. Supporting teachers is a delicate balance of motivating, pushing, challenging, and guiding teachers through processes. You must start with laying the foundation of support by building confidence in teachers and allowing them to be successful. This foundation is creating ways for them to feel good about their work and acknowledging their progress. From there, allow teachers to set goals, high standards, and high expectations to achieve. As they work to achieve the goals they established, have patience to help them improve and develop. Teachers may fall short of their (or your) expectations, but challenge and motivate them to move out of their comfort zones and try new things. Collectively, this is supporting teachers to move from good to great.

Coaching Thought

Best practices are just what the term implies. I can't stress enough that the preceding best practices must be adapted to your environment and culture. Making yourself visible and available, recognizing that we all have differences and different approaches to instruction, maintaining confidentiality, keeping your word, communicating, listening, reflecting, and managing and supporting teachers are all good places to start to lay your foundation to being a great coach. As you gain more experience in your building(s), you will add to this list and create a style of coaching and best practices of your own.

How do you envision these coaching best practices in your coaching role this year?

_____
_____
_____
_____
_____
_____
_____
_____
_____
_____
_____
_____
_____
_____
_____
_____
_____
_____

What are the top instructional coaching mistakes, and how do I avoid them?

Instructional coaching will vary depending on where you are employed, and just as there are best practices of coaching, there are certainly things that coaches just shouldn't do. Since I have experience as a coach in several buildings, I have come up with a baseline of things that coaches shouldn't do.

Don't serve as the principal designee: When you first become an instructional coach, the most important task is to establish trust and a relationship with teachers. Building that relationship means that on multiple occasions, you communicate that you serve as the supporter of teachers. When the principal is out of the building, it's easy for coaches to take over the role because they are not tied to a classroom and can easily make the shift. However, the switch from coach to principal designee can be damaging to your relationships with teachers. Teachers usually see the role of the principal as being an evaluative one. For sake of comparison, imagine a substitute coming into a classroom and "acting" as the classroom's teacher and then leaving a detailed report of what happened in the classroom. The perception of a principal designee is the same; that is, it is interpreted as "tattling" on teachers and staff when the principal returns. After that, the trust is gone, and it's harder to rebuild trust after it's broken than it is to build trust initially. If your principal asks you to take on this role, gently decline and state the above reasons, indicating that you want to protect trust and relationships that were so hard to build.

Don't evaluate teachers: A coach should not serve as the sole evaluator of teachers. If your principal wants to have a hands-off approach with evaluations and giving feedback, and you are the only person who actually sees the teachers teaching, you will be hard-pressed to make much of an impact on your teachers.

Recently, I worked with a coaching client named Jill who had been a classroom teacher, during which time, she had an experience with a new coach, named Ms. Taylor. Ms. Taylor was an aspiring principal and saw her position as a stepping stone and treated the teachers in the building as practice for the big game of being a principal, rather than actually helping them to grow, as she had been entrusted to do.

Jill's first encounter with Ms. Taylor was a bit awkward. Jill brought her class in from recess and found Ms. Taylor standing outside the door holding a clipboard. She barely acknowledged Jill and walked to the back of her classroom to observe what happened next. Jill was a bit surprised and a little annoyed, but assumed she was there to watch the students. As Jill explained the story to me, she said this wasn't the way she had wanted Ms. Taylor to visit her room for the first time. At the end of the lesson, Ms. Taylor left a note on Jill's desk with things she had done well as a teacher and suggestions for ways to improve. Not until then did Jill realize that Ms. Taylor had been there to evaluate her. Jill said it wasn't so much that Ms. Taylor had come and observed her classroom, but the way in which she expressed her concerns and that there was no follow-up to the observation. Ms. Taylor never set a coaching meeting time or even told Jill that she would be coming to observe the classroom to identify a coaching goal.

It took the principal to intervene, as the coach did the same with several teachers throughout the first quarter. Jill talked about how the coach tried to make amends with teachers, but many tuned out when she tried to make suggestions and provide professional development opportunities. The trust was broken before it had a chance to be built. I tell this story because you must not make the mistake of being the evaluator. I believe it's appropriate to watch the teachers teaching to get a sense of their style of teaching and to see which students may need more support. That is a part of our job, but you should do so by appointment, invitation, and with a coaching follow-up meeting, not by surprise. Always make it clear to teachers that you are there to get to know them and their students better, not to evaluate.

<u>Don't be the teachers' classroom assistant:</u> I have run into many roadblocks as an instructional coach with teachers who shy away from me being in their rooms because they simply want me to "prep" lessons for them. There is a balance in helping teachers with their lessons, and I talk about that later in the book.

If a previous (or current) coach in your building has set a precedent in which you run copies and prep materials for teachers to make their lives easier, then you may need your administration's support to help teachers make a shift in how they perceive the role of a coach. You are not necessarily there to make anything easier for anyone. You are there to support teachers in the process of creating the best instructions and learning experiences for students.

Don't be a know it all: Do not come into your position with a big head, believing that you earned this position because of your endless knowledge that cannot be developed further. I have seen coaches who think they have all the answers. Let me be frank. No matter how many degrees or accolades we have, we all can learn something in every situation. Chances are good that you are not an expert on everything your teachers have going on, and acting as if you are will make it difficult for teachers to approach you, for fear you will judge them as being less smart than you are. You are in the place that you are because you know certain things, not everything. You always want to position yourself as being a support and resource for teachers. Remember that not long ago you were a classroom teacher. Be the coach you wanted and needed when you were in the classroom.

Don't expect change too quickly: Do not frustrate yourself and your teachers by expecting them to change too quickly. Just a couple of meetings will not bring radical change for a teacher who is learning something for the first time. We know as teachers that we can't explain the lining up procedure to a class of first graders on the first day of school and then expect them to be experts for the rest of the year, right? It's the same with adults. If you want to push teachers to evaluate data to inform instructional decisions, you may need to model and revisit this concept multiple times, refresh after winter break, and plan to reintroduce it at the beginning of the next year. Eventually, things done often enough become habitual, but you have to practice it enough to get to that point. Don't dismiss teachers as being lazy or as not caring about your ideas because they don't implement them right away. Some learners need a little more time.

Coaching Thought

Keep in mind why you became a coach in the first place—to aide in the improvement of student achievement. It's important that you support teachers through the process and remember that you don't want to do anything to hinder that work.

Think about your time in the classroom. What can you add to preceding concerns that would have made you uncomfortable with a coach? List those and add them to your list of coaching things you *don't* want to do.

_____

_____

_____

_____

_____

_____

_____

_____

_____

_____

_____

_____

_____

_____

_____

_____

_____

How can I be reflective to become a better instructional coach?

The best way to find out what you did well as a coach and where your teachers lacked support is to simply ask them! It can be scary to open yourself up for feedback, but it really is a necessary evil if we are serious about improving ourselves. Keep the survey anonymous, and don't make it a requirement. The end of the year is already stressful enough, and if you force teachers to provide feedback when they don't want to, you will most likely end up with short responses that do not help you. Leave it to the people who feel strongly about you as a coach to give you feedback! You will know their words are sincere. I recommend to keep it anonymous because doing so will prevent teachers from shying away from saying something difficult, and it will keep you from feeling differently about teachers if they do.

Following are a few things to do when you seek feedback from your teachers.

When you send out requests for feedback, make sure you are respectful of your teachers' time. As we all know, education is a whirlwind field with "to do" lists that can stretch for miles. Most people will have no problem completing the survey for you. When you invite the teachers to take your survey, make sure you give them a purpose such as:

"In order to ensure we are maximizing our effectiveness as a team, I would like you to take this quick survey. It's important to me to know what I can do to better serve you and your students as well as what I am doing well. I value your feedback and look forward to seeing your suggestions!"

Make sure you set a reasonable deadline. You don't want to give people too much time, but you also don't want to rush them. Allow about a week for them to complete a survey, which will ensure that it doesn't get buried in an email somewhere. While time is important, so is anonymity. As I mentioned, allow your teachers to give you anonymous feedback; this helps ensure the feedback you get is meaningful. SurveyMonkey and Google Forms are free tools you can use to allow teachers to be anonymous.

When you create your survey, make sure you have open-ended questions. You don't want just a "yes" or "no" option because that doesn't do much to help you. Try to phrase questions so teachers can rate your performance on a scale of 1 to 5, with one being strongly disagreed and five being strongly agreed. After each question, create a space for comments so your teachers can explain their rating.

You can ask any range of questions that will help you grow as an instructional coach. When I create surveys, I tend to ask myself, "What is my goal as an instructional coach?" Naturally, I want to help teachers reach their professional goals by providing them with resources and conducting valuable observations. I also know that in order to be effective, I need to have a good relationship with teachers.

Here are some sample questions you could ask using the 1 to 5 scale:

- My instructional coach communicates regularly with me.
- My instructional coach gives me the opportunity to provide input into activities and programs led by my instructional coach.
- My instructional coach helps me overcome barriers to teaching and learning.
- My instructional coach leads me in evaluating my instruction and curricular programs.
- My instructional coach uses information about student performance to help me improve my instruction.
- My instructional coach helps me to identify and solve problems.
- My instructional coach introduces me to new ways to do things better.
- My instructional coach contributes positively to the improvement of my instruction.
- My instructional coach believes in celebrating instructional and academic improvement.
- My instructional coach maintains confidentiality between us.
- My instructional coach communicates information clearly and concisely.
- My instructional coach maintains open, two-way communication with me.
- My instructional coach assists in developing appropriate student assessments.
- My instructional coach communicates the importance of focusing on the needs of students.
- My instructional coach conducts planning, modeling, and feedback sessions with me.

- My instructional coach helps to create a school environment conducive to increasing achievement.
- My instructional coach works with me to ensure that program standards, instruction, and measures of learning are aligned.
- My instructional coach assists me in instructional planning.
- My instructional coach models research-based instructional procedures and helps me to implement these procedures.
- My coach has helped me perform better.
- My coach has helped me reach my professional goals.
- My observations and feedback have helped me grow as a teacher.
- I have gained helpful resources from my coach.
- I trust my coach.
- I feel I can ask my coach for resources.

By asking a combination of questions, you are hitting all realms of your duties as an instructional coach. Teachers will appreciate you taking the time to get their thoughts and opinions and will be glad to take time out of their busy day to help you grow in your profession.

In addition to the survey, create some questions that you yourself need to answer.

Here are a few that I use at the end of each year:

Specifically, identify what went well this year (e.g., coaching cycles, PD delivery, team building, relationship building).

What changes do I need to make next school year (e.g., coaching cycles, PD delivery, team building, relationship building)?

How will I better connect with my teachers?

Identify teachers with whom I need to have better partnerships.

What areas do I want to grow in professionally and personally?

How do I want next year to be different?

What do I intentionally need to do to make that happen? (Create a Checklist/Implementation Plan.)

Additionally, keeping a reflection journal throughout the year can help you as you prepare for your next year. Reading back through your thoughts over the course of the year about what went well and what did not will provide you with a lot of self-development information. There are likely successes and failures that you forgot about in the busyness of the year, and it's smart to jot them down as they happen.

Coaching Thought

Coaching Remember that feedback is a gift and reflecting is a necessity for improvement. By combining your survey results, your personal reflection questions and answers, and your reflection journal, you will be able to create a data-driven plan of action that will make you a stronger and more refined instructional coach each school year.

How will you conduct reflection surveys this school year? One survey, at the end? One at the beginning? Or three times a year? Write out your plan for reflection.

_____

_____

_____

_____

_____

_____

_____

_____

_____

_____

_____

_____

_____

_____

_____

_____

_____

_____

_____

How can I manage my time as an instructional coach?

One of the biggest struggles in life is not having enough time in a day. This holds true when you are an instructional coach. As I said before, when I first became an instructional coach, I was all over the place. I was trying to get things done, trying not to forget to complete something, and answering an email or attending a meeting. It became very clear that I needed to create a system to manage my time more effectively. My system involved me dedicating a day to planning, mapping out each moment of the day and making sure that I included time to work and time to meet with others. When I was in the classroom, I did my lesson plans on Sunday afternoons. This was the time my children did their homework. I washed clothes and got to the nuts and bolts of preparing for my week. When I became a coach, I thought those days were over, but I soon figured out that I had traded lesson planning for weekly schedule planning on Sunday afternoons.

Over the years, I have developed a few good time management techniques that have worked on a typical day of coaching. You will find that most days present interruptions—it's just the "fun" part of being an instructional coach. Time management becomes a struggle for many coaches because many people in the building view an instructional coach's day as being flexible and wide open. What they don't understand is that you wear many hats and with each of those hats comes a different type of responsibility; therefore, your time is not your own.

The first time management technique I utilized was to plan out each minute of the day. I personally plan out my weekly time from 6 a.m. to 6 p.m. each day. This helps me stay on track even when I have something to do with my children after work. Having a place to be, a focus, or an appointed time to complete a task helps in this regard. I'm sure you know the feeling of coming to work in the morning ready to conquer the world but then get lost in the shuffle and become unproductive because you couldn't remember what it was you were supposed to be doing and how long you thought it would take.

The second time management technique I use is time-blocking. I assign different portions of the day to different things. I am not afraid to communicate my plans to others. If you are interrupted often, it's not a bad thing to let people know that you are currently busy with something, but you will be happy to meet them on a different day or at a different time. When it comes to my principal, I make sure that we meet at the beginning of the year and set the expectation that I have protected time in my schedule each week. This protected time is when I have PLCs, teacher modeling, teacher observations, and overall things I just can't miss. It is wrong to schedule a time to observe teachers implementing strategies they have developed and then not show up. If you don't show up, teachers will lose trust in you, and your hard-earned relationships with them will be lost. It is important for your administration team to understand this early on.

The third time management technique I use is setting a timer. There is something about the pressure of a timer that makes people work a little faster. Add in a small reward, too. "If I get the next three slides of my presentation done in the fifteen minutes that I have, I will get a soda from the vending machine." "If I respond to every email in my inbox in the next twenty minutes, I will make myself some coffee." Those little rewards and the pressure of time work so many wonders. Often you finish more than you set out to do, and you get a nice treat in the middle of your work day!

The fourth time management technique I use is to conduct weekly reflections and set weekly goals. I know this isn't a typical "management" technique, but for me it is a necessity. In order to be efficient in my weekly planning, I must reflect on where I have been to know where I am going. This helps me manage the time I spend to get things done and reflect on whether I need to assign more or less time for certain tasks in the future. If I didn't accomplish all of my goals the previous week, I can discern why and how I can rearrange my schedule to ensure that the next week I accomplish all my goals. Everything else I do can be centered around working toward those goals.

The fifth time management technique I use is to make a weekly schedule. I have found that one of the hardest things an instructional coach does is find time in the day for everything that needs to be done. A great way to do this is by creating your calendar.

Coaching Thought

Time management is a difficult part of life. With only twenty-four hours in a day, it can seem like we never get a chance to rest. So it is important to use your time effectively and implement strategies that will work for you.

Write out how you will incorporate these time management strategies into your instructional coaching role.

_____
_____
_____
_____
_____
_____
_____
_____
_____
_____
_____
_____
_____
_____
_____

How do I become an organized coach?

What you must organize will depend on what your specific duties and assignments are as a coach in your building. Coaching does not have a consistent job description, which makes it tough to feel organized and always put together. So, as you are creating organizational systems for yourself, make sure they are not too rigid. Whatever you are being called upon to do today will likely change in a few weeks—another fun part of the job.

When I work with coaches, I have them set up a basic coaching system. You should do the same. It is never too late to start getting organized. Creating a coaching system will help you become organized, regardless of your duties. This will become your center focus for your organization. When I say "coaching system," I tend to get a lot of blank looks or people acting like I'm crazy.

The coaching system is the way you will collect and manage your records from observations, walk-throughs, feedback, next steps, and so on. I recommend two main types of coaching systems:

Binder system: This is exactly what it sounds like. You use a binder to track your records. (If you are a paper/pencil/pen/marker person, this system is perfect for you!) First, find yourself a two-inch binder. Then insert the same number of dividers as the number of teachers you directly coach and track. Be sure to label each divider with the teacher's name. In each section, place an observation tracker. When you meet with a teacher, you simply record the date and time, what you were looking for in your observations, and what you actually observed. Just quick notes here, not the entire write-up. Be sure to include the date and time of your next meeting, as well as what your focus will be in that meeting. These notes will allow you to detect trends as you continue to coach the teacher. Is he/she continuing to have issues with classroom management? Are his/her lessons falling flat for his/her students? After the observation is complete, place the observation form, your planner from your debrief session, and any other documentation you might have in the binder. The binder is your comprehensive tracking system.

Electronic system: This is also exactly what it sounds like. You use a computer to track your records. On your computer, create a new folder and call it "Coaching Binder" or something similar that is easy for you to find and reference. Within this master folder, create a subfolder for each teacher you coach and name each subfolder according to the related teacher's name. Next, create an Excel spreadsheet or a Google spreadsheet to serve as your tracker. Within the sheet, create a page (tab) for each teacher. At the top of the sheet, create the titles for the various sections—this will resemble the sections in a paper binder. For each, include columns for date, time, subject, what you were looking for and what you saw, the next meeting date, and what your conversation will focus on when you next meet with a teacher. This will allow you to see whether any trends need to be addressed. After each observation, save an electronic copy of your sheet to the related teacher's folder. You will also need to save any other electronic documentation, as well as your debrief notes in the folders so all of this information is easy for you to access. This online binder is a comprehensive tracking system.

Creating these "filing/tracking" systems is only the beginning. Now you are ready to utilize a weekly planner to help organize your time. Note that, as with your binder organizational system, you can choose between a paper or an electronic weekly calendar, whichever works better for you. The goal is keeping yourself organized so you can be the most effective coach possible.

After years of purchasing tons of expensive planners not made for instructional coaches, I created a planner that helps me with every aspect of my coaching. Here are a few things I use my planner for and why.

#1 Track professional development courses attended and presented: Since I have my planner readily available on my desk, I make sure that I record all professional development (PD) courses or seminars I attended throughout the school year. This comes in handy when I need to produce hours for my license, or even if my principal needs to know whether I have already attended a PD course on a specific topic. I also jot down all the PD topics I have presented. This helps when I am planning topics for future PDs, know if I need to follow up on a topic, observe teachers implementing a strategy, and so on.

<u>#2 Identify resources needed or desired for the year:</u> Many times throughout the year, I am sitting in a PD seminar or a meeting when someone talks about a new product or resources that I want to purchase. If you are anything like me, you will jot it down somewhere and never look back. But months later, that resource will pop back up in your head and you will not remember what it was called. Now I have the perfect solution. When a teacher or presenter talks about a resource I want, I put it on a page in my planner. I review the page every so often, do my research on the products/resources, and go from there. This page also gives me in a glance, a "must-have" answer when my family asks, "What do you want for a gift?"

<u>#3 Keep track of teacher birthdays:</u> When I was in the classroom, I used to put all my students' names on a "birthday" poster in my room. Each month we celebrated students' birthdays, and I provided each student with a pencil or pen (depending on the grade level that year), birthday certificate, and a treat. Now that I coach teachers, it's no different. I record each teacher's birthdays (not the year . . . that would get too messy LOL), and I make sure to provide them with a cute handwritten note and something special from me. This year, my daughter and I are making cute Hershey's Kisses bags. I grab a small bag and tissue paper from the Dollar Store and a bag of Hershey's Kisses from the grocery store. At the beginning of each month, I review the birthday list, we create the bags, and they are ready to go! Sometimes I pass them out on the day of the person's birthday; sometimes I pass them out to everyone during the first week of the month. It just depends on how busy the month will be.

<u>#4 Keep track of testing and testing needs:</u> Testing is a part of everyone's vocabulary. Whether we agree or disagree about how it is used, it is one thing we all have in common in the education world. No matter what type of school we work in, we test, in some schools more than others. In the schools in which I have worked, we test a lot. Beginning of the year, middle of the year, end of the year, district test, NWEA, state test, monthly test, you name it, we give it. As an instructional coach, I sometimes organize the testing and sometimes I give the test. To keep up with the dates of the testing windows, I created a page where I track all of the testing, which grade-levels test, which teachers will be testing, and so on. This allows me to stay abreast of what's happening when I create my weekly schedules.

#5 Develop and track SMART professional coaching goals for yourself each term (4): Setting goals helps us stay focused and work on improvement. For my evaluation, I have to set a professional goal for the school year. I have found that in order for me to reach that yearly goal, I need to break the goal down into smaller goal action steps throughout the school year. Many times, we set the beginning of the year goals with great intentions, but throughout the year, our actions have nothing to do with our overall goal. So I like to set a goal each quarter that will help me to reach my yearly professional goal. Of course, the goal is a SMART goal, and I reflect each quarter to make sure I am on the right track. If I am, I can set my next goal for the next quarter. If I am not, I reflect on why I didn't reach the goal and set a new goal based on that.

#6 Track monthly coaching cycles for eight teachers per month: In my big binder/electronic system, I keep all of my coaching documents and my official forms. In my planner, I have a quick form to help me assess my coaching cycles for the month. This allows me to do a quick reflection when I am working with a teacher to see growth. This also allows me to give my administration enough information to know exactly who I am working with and what the focus is, but not all the deep details. We coaches walk a thin line between keeping a teacher's trust and revealing too much to the administration. If my principal asks for a monthly coaching report, I can easily submit this form and be in compliance.

#7 Create weekly coaching goals and planning: When I was in the classroom, I knew exactly what standards I needed to teach and for what subjects each week. It was how I began my lesson plans. With coaching, understanding what needs to be done each week works the same way. You have to know what you will be doing before you can set a schedule. I use this form to identify my coaching goals for the week. There may be testing, an all-school assembly, or professional development. I look at all factors and create a list of goals—how many teachers' classrooms I will visit, how many coaching cycles I will complete, and so on. Setting goals for the week allows me to stay on track and get things done. With coaching, you can become easily sidetracked.

#8 Reflect weekly on coaching goals: Yes, I am a BIG reflector. Before I set goals for the upcoming week, I have to see what I accomplished the previous week. Did I hit my goals? If I didn't, why not? How can I get better? Did I plan too much or not enough? If I didn't complete my weekly goals, they may get pushed to the next week, but I have thought about why they were not completed and how I can ensure that they will be completed the next week.

#9 Keep track of meetings attended, and notes, and next steps: As a coach, you attend a ton of meetings. I know personally, I have my admin meeting, teacher meetings, data meetings, walking down the hall meetings, and many more. I have a notebook in which I keep notes of my regularly scheduled meetings, but sometimes (more than I would like), I am pulled into a meeting and don't have my notebook with me. Having a set space to jot down notes from an unplanned meeting is important. I take those notes and transfer them, if necessary. If not, I still have a record of what we talked about and any next steps needed. This comes into play with my "Weekly Goals" if next steps are warranted.

#10 Create a schedule each day—Sunday through Saturday from 6:00 a.m. to 6:00 p.m.: Most people think being a coach means no more lesson plans. Well, this is not entirely true. Each week, just like lesson planning, you must create a schedule from the time you walk in the door to the time you walk out. Having a plan like this makes for an impactful and effective coach. When I say plan it out, I mean plan it out! All the way from morning duty to open office hours to lunch and lunch duty. I have something scheduled for each minute of the day. This helps me to stay focused, get things done, and hold others accountable for requesting my time.

I currently work in a 9–12 building. I have worked in K–8, K–6, and 7–12, and I have been responsible for only one subject area each year. This year, I am responsible for working with all teachers. So it is very important that I make a tight schedule and stick to it. Now, I know there are things that come up each week, and in my schedule, I leave open slots to move things around a bit, mostly on Thursdays and Fridays. But those open times are also for when a teacher wants to meet but we didn't have it planned, and I just tell the teacher that this is the time I am open.

My principals in the past sometimes called me randomly and asked me to meet with them. If the meetings could wait, through experience, I learned to let them know exactly when I had an opening to meet. If the meeting couldn't wait, then I moved what I was currently doing into an open slot. As I mentioned earlier, I let my principals know upfront that I have protected time in my schedule, time that I use to observe a teacher during a cycle, or to schedule a co-teach, or for a debrief meeting. I make it very clear that these times must be respected in order for me to achieve the full outcome of my coaching. You want to try to ensure that you and your principal agree to such matters at the beginning of the school year. This way, throughout the year, you will only have to give the principal a gentle reminder.

#11 Track any personal/home to-dos: I have a personal planner I use for my family activities, but I like to have a place where I can put something that I need to take care of on my break or right after school. If I have to email my kids' coach or teacher, pay a bill, or leave early due to my kids' early dismissal, I try to make sure I put it in the work planner that I access daily. This is very beneficial when planning my time for the week. If I know I have to leave an hour early to pick up one of the kids, I put that in the weekly schedule.

#12 Track weekly teacher communication: Many times I am stopped in the hallway by teachers asking me if I can send them something quickly. Having a place to jot down those notes is perfect so I don't forget. You will need a place like this. Teachers will stop and ask you for things more than you could ever imagine.

Coaching Thought

The key to being an effective and impactful coach is organization. I am way more organized in my work life than I am in my personal life. Make sure you create a system that allows you to store documents for tracking purposes and create a planner that works for you. There are a ton of options out there. Planning and reflecting each week will help you feel confident and ready as a coach, and your teachers will love you for it.

What type of system will I use? What will my weekly planner look like? Why did I choose a particular system?

_____

_____

_____

_____

_____

_____

_____

_____

_____

_____

_____

_____

_____

_____

_____

How do I set up and create an instructional coaching schedule?

During my first instructional coaching position, my schedule was a hot mess of sticky notes on my desk (well, the sticky note part is still the same; I should buy stock in Post-it) and scrolling through my inbox to make sure I hadn't missed anything. I was so busy with everything that I hadn't taken the time to sit down and create a proper schedule, and I know that it negatively impacted the efficiency of my work.

As a classroom teacher, one of the expectations is that you will create weekly lesson plans for your students. Having the planning and prep done upfront ensures that you are familiar with the material and ready to deliver it in a dynamic way. As a coach, your weekly plan will look different, but the focus is the same. You need to plan in order to most effectively create change and success for your teachers. Rather than lesson planning, you will be mapping out a scheduled plan of how you are going to help the teachers you support in becoming more effective in the classroom. Your plan will need to include those you will work with, the goals for them, as well as how you intend to work toward those goals. Not only does weekly planning provide a roadmap for your week (both for you and for others who need to see how they fit into your schedule), it also shows that you are prepared with materials that enable you to be efficient in your role as coach.

I know that developing a weekly coaching plan sounds daunting, so I have developed an eight-step plan to help you plan out your weekly coaching schedule. These steps are helpful whether this is the first weekly schedule you have made as a coach or if you've been at this for years, but are needing a fresh start. Steps 1–4 are done for the initial setup of your weekly schedule, and steps 5–8 are done every week to ensure you are totally ready for that week.

Step 1: Decide on the planning format you want to use, that is, electronic or paper, as previously discussed. If you choose to use a paper planning format, print a weeklong planning template (and a backup or two!). If you are planning to use an electronic template, you will have to choose what platform you want to work with. (Excel, Google Sheets, etc.). Google Sheets as well as Outlook are both updated in real time, which makes sharing them with colleagues via email ideal, as they will always see the most updated version.

Step 2: Make a list of all recurring weekly activities.

For example:
- Arrival and Dismissal Duty
- Lunch Duty
- Weekly Coach + Principal Meeting
- Grade Level meeting
- PLCs
- Staff Development Meetings
- Daily Office Hours

If activities happen weekly, put them on this list!

Note: I want to make sure that you understand what office hours means. As a coach, your office hours is your planning period. Do not skip out on your office hours! While the time of your office hours might change, be sure to schedule your time and KEEP your time. You will have a lot of documentation to cover, not to mention creating and tweaking the various plans you have with each of the teachers you are coaching. Office hours are vital to maintaining a healthy work and home balance, which is vital to being an effective coach. Burn out isn't going to do you or your teachers any favors!

Step 3: Enter time slots into your weekly planner. If you are an elementary teacher, I recommend using fifteen-minute increments in your plan. It will be tedious to set up, but the more detailed your schedule is, the more organized you will feel as you go through your week. Many elementary classrooms run on different schedules, so being more refined in your times will serve you well. If you coach middle or high school, I recommend organizing the time according to your school's periods—Period 1: 8:05–9:00; Period 2: 9:10–10:05, and so on.

Step 4: Insert your recurring activities (the list you made in Step 2) into your weekly template.

Step 5: Consult your school or building calendar and enter any special events into your template. Add events like staff meetings, professional development days, holidays, school assemblies, teacher workdays, conferences, or any other school-wide activity that will consume your required classroom minutes. Do this every week!

Step 6: Now it's time to fill in the open slots on your calendar. For this, you want to keep in mind the different tiers of support you have for teachers. You will meet with some teachers weekly, some quarterly, some in a cycle, and some you will meet individually and in a group; you get the idea. On top of that, keep in mind the teachers' various classroom schedules and make sure they are available at the time you assign to meet with them. This process will take the most time and be the most tedious! It is also one of the most important steps you can take and needs to be done upfront to keep it moving all week long.

Be sure to write the reason for scheduling activities in your planning template as well as the person you are meeting with and the time (e.g., Turner–Observation Entry Procedure or Jackson–Observation Debrief from math lesson). This way you will know exactly why you scheduled the time and you will be able to better prepare for activity. The whole point of your weekly schedule is to be prepared for the week ahead so that things move along as smoothly as possible.

Step 7: In Step 2, you created a weekly schedule of daily office hours. Now that the rest of the schedule is filled, you need to go back and enter what you are planning to do during those office hours. For example: You are observing Turner on Tuesday at 8:40 for Entry Procedures, and your debrief is scheduled for Wednesday at 9:20. You have office hours on Tuesday from 2:20–3:20. This is when you will plan your debrief meeting, so you will put Turner Debrief Prep in your schedule. You will want to do this with all of your observations, debriefs, testing schedules, data reviews, and so on. If you keep your day scheduled, you are more likely to get all of your work done during work hours, thus maintaining that elusive work–life balance we talked about. Trust me! Learn from me—you know I learned all of this the hard way.

Step 8: The final step! The last thing you need to do (every week) is to go back through your weekly schedule and add topics for the meetings you have scheduled. In Step 2, you entered PLCs, staff development meetings, grade level meetings, and so forth. Now is the time to go through the schedule and enter what you hope to discuss at the meetings. Also, be sure to note whether you are hosting the meetings or need to have materials or documents prepared for the meetings. If you do, schedule a time to perform those tasks during your office hours. Are you sensing a theme here? Write everything down. The more detailed you are, the easier your workflow will be. Pat yourself on the back! You have scheduled your first week.

Coaching Thought

Plan every minute of your time. This will enable you to be efficient. Planning is not optional! If you fail to plan, you plan to fail. You want to be as efficient as possible, as you will be wearing many different hats in one day, and you want to do it with a smile. Planning allows you to work ahead and will help you stay ahead of your stress.

Write your nonnegotiables and which extras you want in your planner. Decide the type of planner you want and then can start looking for one.

_____

_____

_____

_____

_____

_____

_____

_____

_____

_____

_____

_____

_____

_____

_____

_____

_____

How can I create my coaching philosophy?

Your coaching philosophy is similar to your teaching philosophy, because at the end of the day, you are there to help teachers so that students can grow. The only difference between your classroom teaching days and now is that your goal before was to find a way to help each child in your classroom grow whereas now you have the opportunity to help teachers help students all over your school grow!

Developing a coaching philosophy is what helps you determine the kind of instructional coach you will be. Your instructional coaching philosophy should include three things: (1) your why, (2) the instructional coaching values you have established for yourself, and (3) your leadership style. Together, these form your instructional coaching philosophy.

(1) Your Why? Either you were asked to become an instructional coach or you applied. Either way, you are now in the role. You need to establish your why for choosing to be an instructional coach. Why did you accept the position? Was it to provide a positive experience for teachers needing help? Was it to expand your reach in helping more students in your building? Was it to help teachers reach their full potential? Answering these questions will help you discover why you are coaching.

(2) Your instructional values: Coaches must develop core values for the work they do. According to Yourdictionary.com, core values are the fundamental beliefs of a person or organization. These guiding principles dictate behavior and can help people understand the difference between right and wrong. Core values also help companies determine whether they are on the right path and fulfilling their goals by creating an unwavering guide. I completed an exercise my third year of coaching that allowed me to develop my coaching values. Visit the website https://www.cmu.edu/career/documents/my-career-path-activities/values-exercise.pdf and follow the steps to create your coaching values.

Here are my coaching values, which you can use as a guide to developing yours.

Equity

As a coach

- I am responsive to the situational needs of each of my teachers.
- I have high expectations for all the teachers I work with.
- I understand and apply the knowledge I know about adult development in my coaching.

High Expectations

As a coach

- I create a mindset and exhibit actions that suggest a partnership that is grounded in respect.
- I build trust with the positive intent to coach without judgment.
- I hold no negative presuppositions about the teachers I coach.
- I believe that all teachers can grow and learn.
- I ensure that I stay abreast of best practices in professional learning.
- I always consider data to make decisions.

Collaboration

As a coach

- I am energizing and rejuvenating to teachers.
- I work together with the teacher(s) and share ideas.
- I work together toward a common goal, in an inclusive and trusting environment.
- I work effectively alongside and with teachers and principals.

Communication

As a coach

- I respond to the professional needs of teachers in a timely and authentic manner.
- I have empathy.
- I build interpersonal relationships.
- I encourage others.
- I look at situations from a positive perspective.
- I use active listening skills.
- I help teachers and principals to view situations from a different perspective.

Reflection

As a coach

- I have reflective dialogue that provides opportunities for growth by supporting a process of reflection and adjustment of my practice.
- I engage in a reflective cycle that includes questioning, planning, implementing, and reflecting that is rooted a growth mindset.
- I lead teachers to reflect for the growth of students and teachers.
- I am reflective about my own practices.
- I have a passion for ongoing development for myself and teachers.

(3) <u>Your leadership style:</u> Instructional coaches are considered teacher leaders and must incorporate a style of leadership that will be supportive to the teachers they are coaching. Visit this website and complete the six steps to discover your leadership style: <u>https://www.skillsyouneed.com/lead/develop-leadership-style.html</u>.

My leadership style is "servant leadership." I believe in being a servant to my teachers first. I know the word "servant" may seem a bit odd, but I use the word to mean that I will provide teachers with the knowledge and resources they need to be successful. By doing so, I am leading them to improve instruction for students.

Coaching Thought

In order to be effective in your role, it's important to create a guide and philosophy that you can stand by when things get fuzzy. By pulling all three parts together, you develop that guide.

Here is my instructional coaching philosophy statement:

> My instructional coaching philosophy stresses the importance of, equity, high expectations, collaboration, communication, and reflection (**Values**). I believe in being a servant to my teachers first by providing them with the knowledge and resources they need to be successful (**Leadership style**) to improve instruction for all students (**Purpose**).

Using the example, create your own philosophy.

_____
_____
_____
_____
_____
_____
_____
_____
_____
_____
_____
_____
_____
_____

What does goal setting look like when you are a coach?

Just as you encourage your teachers to do when setting goals, make SMART goals for yourself that are measurable so you will know when you've met them. You can set large goals for the year, along with several smaller goals that will serve as benchmarks to keep you on track. Make sure that you create professional development goals for yourself as well as goals that align to the improvement goals for the school.

A few years ago, my school implemented the PLC model for the first time. So I will use the PLC implementation process for illustration. Since I was rolling out the PLC model for the first time in my building, I set the SMART goal, "100% of content teams will be engaged and conducting PLCs by the end of the year." That was definitely measurable. But I had a team that didn't buy into the PLC model by the end of the year, and they weren't following the PLC process, and I didn't meet my goal. I was fine with not meeting my goal because I had achieved 90 percent of it. However, as I reflected, I realized that if I had decided to reset that goal, I would have thought through the goal-setting process and taken into account that there will always be people who are resistant to change, and I would have set my goal to include that factor.

In the beginning of the school year, I created benchmark goals along the way:

1. All teams have developed norms and established a meeting time and place for PLC by fall break.

2. Teachers are taking pretest and post-test data at least once per unit by winter break.

3. Teachers have established a routine for re-teaching skills their students did not master on a regular basis by spring break.

4. Students have created charts of skills that will need to be reinforced at the beginning of the next grade level before the end of the year.

Creating benchmark goals allowed me to monitor my implementation and support throughout the year and gave me a red flag if I needed to make some adjustments.

The example I gave is a goal that was connected to the improvement goal for the building. I also set a professional development goal to increase my knowledge in the area of student-centered coaching by conducting four student coaching cycles with two teachers by the end of the school year. I was able to document this goal by coaching cycle documentation and my notes from reading the books by Diane Sweeney, mentioned earlier.

To ensure that you set goals that will support your growth as a coach, revisit the preceding goals and reassess on them. Did you meet your goals? Did you surpass them and then set new goals? Did you fall a little short? Reflect on the challenges you met and the successes you had. Keeping a journal throughout the year can help with this, or you can keep detailed notes about all of your PLCs, data meetings, coaching cycles, and PD sessions and read through all of your notes at the end of the year. What was a struggle that you'd like to handle better the next school year? What resources are there to help you in this area? Make it your summer mission to learn a little bit more about your areas of weakness.

Coaching Thought

Setting goals as a coach is no different than setting goals as a teacher. If you are setting goals and reflecting back to see how you did and where you can improve, you will always grow.

If this is your first year as a coach, think about some professional goals you would like to create for the upcoming school year and write a few here. If you are a coach who has some experience, do some reflecting about your last year of coaching and make a list of a few things you want to work on. During your beginning of the year meeting with your principal or admin team, ask about the school initiatives and be sure to create an improvement goal that will support your school's or district's improvement goal.

_____
_____
_____
_____
_____
_____
_____
_____
_____
_____
_____
_____
_____

Part III

Supporting Your Teachers

"When teachers stop learning, so do students"

- Jim Knight

How can I create an environment of support for teachers?

Creating an environment of support sets the tone for teachers to feel comfortable enough to want to come and meet with you. If coaching is new to the school or you are a new coach, it will take time for teachers to feel you out and understand your role. They are not sure exactly who you are and what you stand for. That's where you start with building trust. If you offer support, demonstrate care, show confidence, keep a teacher's perspective, and maintain confidentiality, you will be on your way to opening the door for coaching in your building.

Let's look at these five pieces to this puzzle more closely.

Offer support: Reach out to teachers equitably, but don't be surprised if some don't respond. Keep reaching out to all, but feed the hungry. Don't take offense if not everyone is receptive. In addition, take some time to really pay attention to teachers' instructions and conversations while in class or in meetings. Jot down a few notes about the teachers' confidence and frustrations. This can help when planning a feedback session where you will have the perfect opportunity to provide the right coaching intervention. During your one-on-one meetings, give the teachers the opportunity to confirm your perception by asking open questions. This will allow teachers to open up and feel like you care and want to know more about their point of view.

Demonstrate care: Each morning in the early weeks of each semester, I stop by each teacher's room and say "Good Morning" and ask "Is there something I can help you with this morning?" Teachers will start to see you as a support and not judgmental.

Show confidence: I have found that praising teachers for the small things boosts confidence and creates a bond between me and them. Being intentional with the praise before big successes happen will support the development of a growth mindset and encourage responsibility. Many times I ask teachers to try something new in their classrooms. I have learned that teachers need opportunities to consider and evaluate possibilities, and through dialogue, receive affirmation and confirmation about actions taken and results achieved.

This process helps them sort through what is working and what is not and sets them up for their next steps, which again helps to build confidence. Giving honest praise, thoughtful responses, and supportive feedback creates a strong environment of caring and comfort for the teacher.

Keep perspective: Never forget what it was like to be in the classroom. Sometimes, administrators and coaches add to teachers' plates tons of things that need to be completed. Yes, they are a priority, but so is a teacher's sanity. Classroom teachers are at the forefront of instruction. They are the ones who deliver the information to the students. We all know that teaching can be hard and stressful. We can plan lessons, practice for days, and when we are delivering, it can all go wrong. Be cautious of those efforts and remember what it was like for you as a teacher. Being humble and remembering will build an open, caring environment for when teachers are truly frustrated and confused and really need your help. They will most likely be open to you.

Maintain confidentiality: I know I spoke about this previously, but I want to be clear that a coach's job walks a thin line each day. It is important to set a code of ethics for yourself. Coaches must maintain confidentiality, not only in talking with other teachers but also in their conversations with administrators. Coaches who are seen as being untrustworthy have difficulty convincing a teacher that they are there to support the teacher with instruction. Coaches who talk to others about what they have seen in classrooms or what they think about a specific teacher will not be welcomed as a colleague, which will make the coaching role that much harder.

Coaching Thought

Coaching begins with the end in mind. The end is to get teachers to improve instruction for students. The beginning means that you have to open the door to coaching by setting the stage to build trust and allow room for teachers to feel vulnerable enough to accept the help. It will not always be easy, but it will be worth it.

When starting out the year, think about the five things mentioned above and how you can ensure that these points are incorporated from the beginning.

_____
_____
_____
_____
_____
_____
_____
_____
_____
_____
_____
_____
_____
_____

How will I identify which teachers need support?

This is different for each coach and is based on the model your district is using. The districts I've worked in have used the model in which everyone gets a coach and where coaches are content-specific. In my work with coaches, I have learned that other districts allow for teachers to volunteer to be coached, whereas if there is a teacher improvement plan (this has many names), a coach is required.

There are three different approaches to identifying a teacher who needs coaching.

The first approach is one in which everyone gets a coach, which means that you will support all teachers in your building. You will need to tier your teachers for support and give new teachers and struggling teachers intensive support and other teachers mid-level support. All teachers will complete coaching cycles.

The second approach is the teacher volunteer model. Teachers will ask for your support in implementing something they saw during a professional development session, a new district, a school building initiative, or something they are just struggling with. You will provide each teacher with a menu of offerings and provide school-wide professional development. The teacher will initiate one-on-one meetings.

The third approach is the admin referral model. Teachers will be required to complete a coaching cycle(s) with you based on a goal that is set by the administration.

Coaching Thought

Regardless of the way in which a teacher is inducted into your coaching program, be sure to keep documentation of your coaching cycles. Some cycles may be more informal than others, especially when teachers volunteer to be coached. Keeping documentation will protect you, and it's also data to support your work.

Ask your administrator which approach your school supports. Then write it out here so that you know how to approach your coaching.

_____
_____
_____
_____
_____
_____
_____
_____
_____
_____
_____
_____
_____
_____
_____
_____

How do I best provide meaningful feedback for teachers?

When you were a classroom teacher, feedback was probably something you heard emphasized in a professional development session, staff meeting, or perhaps in an observation. The conversation was always around the topic of "there are right and wrong ways to provide feedback to a student that they will internalize as positive and grow from." As an instructional coach, you can take those same sentiments of giving meaningful feedback to a student and apply them to giving feedback to a teacher when you are coaching them.

When it comes to providing feedback for teachers, you must think of it in two ways. The first way is "immediate feedback." Immediate feedback is provided through walkthroughs or quick observation forms. Normally, this feedback is provided to the teacher immediately and is left on the teacher's desk or chair and, if provided electronically, is sent in an email before you leave the room.

The second way is the "feedback meeting." The feedback meeting usually occurs within forty-eight hours of a classroom visit. This is the time that you, as the instructional coach, will ask the teacher questions, provide specific things for the teacher to complete, and even teach or review a new teaching strategy for the teacher to implement. This meeting is usually a part of the coaching cycle.

Let's first look at the different ways to provide immediate feedback.

We, as instructional coaches, use walkthrough forms. These forms help us to look at specific things when we do a walkthrough. There are two different types of quick walkthroughs.

The first type of walkthrough is a "positive feedback" walkthrough. This type of walkthrough is usually done once a month, but they are not connected to a goal. Positive feedback walkthroughs are done simply to document something good that is happening in the classroom or that the teacher is doing. There are times or situations where these types of walkthroughs may be difficult to do. This makes them all the more important! Just like we all have one of "those" classes in our teaching career, we will have one of "those" teachers in our coaching career. Giving positive feedback is vital to maintaining a good working relationship. No matter what, there is always something we can say that is positive about what a teacher is doing in the classroom.

The second type of walkthrough is a "specific focused" walkthrough. This type of walkthrough is done when you have done a baseline observation and identified a specific goal or goals you and your teacher are working to complete. You can also conduct this type of walkthrough if you have a building-level initiative and want to make sure teachers are implementing the strategies correctly. When you do a specific focused walkthrough, you need to have a clear goal for your observation before you walk into the room. When you go into the room, you could be looking for evidence of student engagement, guided reading, guided math, block instructional execution, the use of specific instructional strategies, such as close reading, learning groups, and so on. You may also be looking for co-teaching models, classroom management, and behavior management. It could even be a follow-up to a new teaching strategy that was taught during the last PLC or professional development session.

Now let's look at the feedback meeting.

When it comes to planning feedback meetings, I have come up with a few items to ensure that I provide teachers with well-balanced feedback. For me, that means it's not all negative or all positive, and it definitely has a balance. In order to make sure that I make it balanced, I include five things in each of my meetings.

#1 I provide precise praise: As always, you want to establish a positive relationship with your teachers. Doing so in the most positive way is the most beneficial for all involved. Whether this is after the first walkthrough or the twentieth, always start your feedback meeting with something that the teacher did well. Again, going back to the conversation of feedback in the classroom, we must remember that just like with kiddos, adults want to feel good about what went well. This will set the tone of the meeting and can make or break what constructive criticism you may need to suggest later. Be specific in your praise. A simple "good job on the lesson today" isn't sufficient.

A teacher needs to hear what you specifically liked. For example, "I noticed that Sam was being disruptive while working in his small group. Instead of making a scene in front of the entire room, I love how you calmly got down next to him and redirected his behavior." Being specific lets teachers know what you liked, and they are more likely to repeat the behavior.

#2 I ask probing questions: If you really want teachers you are coaching to buy into what they can do to improve a lesson, ask questions that, after consideration, they can fully understand and resolve. I have learned from experience that the conversation between a coach and teachers could take a terrible turn if the coach decides to give suggestions about how to change a lesson without the teachers understanding anything needed to be improved. Take some time to plan a few probing questions prior to your meetings. Think about the different ways teachers could answer the questions, and be ready to ask more questions to get teachers to discover what they need to improve. By asking probing questions, teachers are more likely to buy into your ideas and implement change.

#3 I help to identify the problem and take action: By asking probing questions, you enable the teacher to identify what the problem. This will give you the opening you need to help the teacher put practice into action. Teachers who can successfully identify the problem and put steps for improvement into action will continue to be reflective in the coming weeks. If a teacher cannot identify what the problem is, it's the instructional coach's responsibility to positively share what can be done to improve student achievement. Always, always, always put the focus on what can be done to improve student achievement, not on what went wrong with a lesson. By making the students the focal point, teachers may not feel as though they are being attacked.

#4 I Practice with the teachers: I know this may sound a bit crazy. You ask, "Practice? What am I practicing?" You are practicing the strategy for improvement. Just as a teacher does with students, an instructional coach needs to model for teachers. After you and the teacher have identified what needs to be improved, you need to model the role of the teacher while the teacher takes on the role of the student. Now, I must be honest, when it comes to modeling, I have not always been the best. Over the years, I have learned to model for my teachers by using videos of other teachers.

Because I know exactly what I want the teacher to work on and have prompted the teacher to figure it out, prior to the meeting, I search for a video with an example of the strategy "in action." When it's time to "model," I can just press Play. Since I reviewed the video prior to the meeting, I have already noted topics to discuss and questions to ask the teacher during and after the video. If I am comfortable with the strategy and confident of being able to model it, I also use the traditional modeling strategy of role playing. Role playing with teachers is a great modeling tool and allows teachers to practice strategies before delivering the next lesson. This approach gives teachers the confidence they need to perform such that their students' performance improves. Once teachers feel confident they have learned what the coach has modeled, the roles are switched, with the coach being the teachers' imaginary student.

When modeling, I have stopped teachers in action to ask why they did something a particular way. This helps teachers to become aware of their actions and then try to change whatever is not working. Sometimes teachers will repeat an action multiple times until they get it right. Many times, I tell teachers it is "practicing for the play." I ask them, "Would you send students out on the stage to perform without making sure they had mastered their lines?" Teachers always say "no"; as their instructional coach, neither will I.

#5 I plan ahead and follow up: By the end of your meetings with teachers, you and the teachers should have identified the need for improvement, devised a plan, and even practiced and prepared for the lesson. Before you end the meetings, take some time to discuss when teachers will implement the practiced strategy. Then put this information in the lesson plans, discuss a day and time when you can observe the teachers implementing the lessons, and then schedule a meeting time to provide feedback for the newly revised and taught lesson. This time your "specific feedback" will be all about this strategy.

Coaching Thought

As you continue to provide feedback to teachers, look for the positives, stress the importance of staying on top of the latest techniques to improve student achievement, and keep all comments student-centered. Remember, you are all there for students' growth and achievement; therefore, you are on the same team. After all, we are all in this profession because of the kids.

Gather your thoughts on providing feedback. Do you have the correct feedback forms to use when conducting conversations? If so, write the name of each form and what you will use it for. If not, you can visit the Simply Coaching + Teaching (https://simplycoachingandteaching.com) website and check out the available forms. Record which forms you would like to use and what you will use them for.

How can I balance providing resources and help to teachers with teaching them where to find the resources or to try strategies themselves? I often felt like I was simply doing things for teachers, but they were not learning and growing.

This a very common issue that many new and some veteran coaches run into. Building relationships with teachers can be misconstrued, with coaches feeling like they need to be the teachers' personal assistant at times. Coaches might say, "I'll make those copies for you! I'll print those centers for you!" While that is really nice of you, it sets a precedent that is hard to break. Consider this situation: Your plate is full and you are trying to do some really good coaching work in your building, and Ms. Thomas from fifth grade emails you asking if you could help her make some centers for next week. You're going to have to say no, and Ms. Thomas is going to be confused and probably annoyed. But you confused her from the beginning. Instead, at the beginning of the school year, host a meeting with teachers and your administration. Discuss the vision for your role and share what you will be offering teachers. Those are the things you should focus on. If you take the time to tell your teachers what you offer as a coach, don't immediately go against your word by running a bunch of copies for them just so they will like you. I know that may sound a bit harsh, but it's the truth. You will most definitely find yourself in a position before too long where you are too busy to get the centers made, but your teachers no longer remember how to do it themselves.

The fact that we are called coaches is no accident. Think of a baseball coach. How much good would a coach be if he were to spend each practice hitting the ball in front of the players? What if he stood on the pitcher's mound and talked about technique and practiced pitching while his players stood on the field and observed. Would they have a good idea of what their coach knew how to do? Sure. Would they grow as players? Absolutely not. The baseball coach's job is to watch his players doing what they do in their various positions, and then refine their actions to make them better. This may involve them doing some things that are out of their comfort zone, or maybe they need to do some workouts that are a little difficult. But the coach knows that through this discomfort, growth will inevitably happen.

Let's be real. You are not here to make everyone feel comfortable with where they currently stand as a teacher. Yes, you want to go into each room and give a gold star and leave, and yes, you want to do the heavy lifting so everyone likes you. But if you do all that, why do they need a coach? A coach helps teachers see how to differentiate their work, and then lets them do it on their own. A coach observes a teacher and then gives feedback on how to improve in an area. A coach does not make all the classroom copies, cut and set up centers, or write lesson plans alone for a teacher to use.

If you're wondering how to balance the two, my argument would be to never start. Provide coaching, not coddling. If a teacher is struggling with staying on top of her lesson planning demands, and she's working all weekend on making centers and planning small groups, you are not making her a more efficient teacher by swooping in and doing it for her. Help her refine her routines so she is more focused and can work faster. Your job is to educate her so that area is not a struggle any longer.

Coaching Thought

We are teachers first. We remember the classroom and how overwhelming it can be, and when we become coaches we want to always make the classroom job easier. But we must remember that we have to use our experiences in the classroom and our knowledge base to help teachers create systems and routines that will help make things better, but they must do the work. Being a coach is a delicate balance between supporting and doing the work. Choose to help teachers become great, and don't do the work for them.

Create a list of dos and don'ts. These are the things you will do for teachers and things you will not do. You don't have to share this list with anyone. The items on the list are the boundaries you set for yourself, and when making a decision, pull out your list and use it as a reference.

_____

_____

_____

_____

_____

_____

_____

_____

_____

_____

_____

_____

_____

_____

_____

_____

What do I do when I have a teacher who doesn't improve?

My first word of cautionary wisdom here is to make sure you have given a teacher ample time to show growth, and that you are fairly measuring the growth before you decide that he is not improving. Sometimes we have students who are not showing growth the way that we are measuring it: universal screeners, unit tests, state assessments, and so forth. It's frustrating, and you feel like you have poured all your energy into one student only to be spinning your wheels for half of the year. Then his teacher the following year stops you in the hall and says, "Did you have Jake last year? Wow, he has really taken off with fractions. I can tell that you did a great job laying the groundwork last year, because he really understands what a fraction is." Your heart swells, but you also suspect that this teacher is insane, or maybe that you aren't talking about the same Jake.

We know as teachers that all children can learn, but not the same way or on the same day. This is also true for teachers. Sometimes, rather than pounding through coaching cycle after coaching cycle, feeling frustrated that we are seeing the same mistakes, we need to take a step back and let all of our teaching just sink in for a while. Let the teacher navigate her way through without you as a crutch for a little bit, and see what happens. If you take a few weeks off, and come back to observe again, you may be pleasantly surprised at the strategies the teacher adopted when she had to think for herself for a few weeks.

Another factor we need to look at when a teacher is not progressing is our approach to coaching. We must be careful not to pile up too many things for teachers to work on all at once. I have found that if I have a teacher who is not improving, I must stop and evaluate what and how much I am asking the teacher to work on at once. Have I devised a plan of action that maps out a trajectory of improvement? For example, say that I am working with Ms. Jackson on classroom management. I conduct a baseline observation in her classroom and notice that the class is completely out of control. There are no routines in place, no directions being given, no call to actions, no organization, and she is just overwhelmed by it all. In this case, I could meet with Ms. Jackson and have her implement about twelve different things immediately, but she would not be able to keep up and would feel even more overwhelmed. Instead, I choose one to two things she can implement that will have the biggest impact. This approach will allow me to work with Ms. Jackson to implement the strategies and see a small victory. Accomplishing the small victory will allow Ms. Jackson to build confidence about the changes she is making; she will also become accustomed to the new routines, and then we can add more and more as time goes on. We as coaches tend to want to fix everything immediately, but we must remember our time in the classroom. Could you have handled a ton of change all at once?

It is definitely possible that a teacher does not move forward. The reality may be that the teacher doesn't want to grow. The teacher may resist you for cramping her style and encouraging her to shake things up. She may resist the principal for suggesting you work with her. She may be close to retirement and is just counting down the minutes until it's all over (I have experienced this a number of times). Such teachers may be suffering from burnout and exhaustion and are not able to listen to your attempts to improve them, because their minds have checked out.

If none of the above reflects your working relationship with your staff, and you have a teacher who is staunchly staying put, despite what you believe to be a meaningful discussion and feedback about his teaching, it may be time to hand the situation over to administration. However, be cautious about making this decision, and do not take it lightly. This is a teacher for whom you have weeks and weeks of documented coaching that indicates more of a refusal to improve than a slow improvement process. When you have worked and done all you can, then it's time to get administration involved. In this case, perhaps an improvement plan needs to be put in place, or maybe the teacher is severely unhappy in their grade level, or the problem may even stem from the teacher's personal life. Whatever the case, you will be better served to turn the situation over to the principal.

Coaching Thought

Coaching is like teaching in many ways. You have to give your students, or in this case your teachers, time to learn and grow. They must be supported through the process. You will have opportunities to monitor progress and "reteach" the concept over and over. The key is to be a reflective coach. When implementing change, it's not always the teacher who must change; the coach must also be flexible enough to meet the needs of the teacher. When in the classroom, I always took into consideration the different learning styles of my students to make sure that I was meeting everyone's needs, I try to do this as well as a coach. Take an inventory of your teachers' learning styles and think of ways you can meet their needs when helping them learn about and incorporate new strategies. If a teacher is not improving, try to identify the problem and work with the teacher until no options are left; then go to the administration for guidance and direction.

Google "Learning Styles Survey" and examine the different surveys. From those surveys, you can map out a quick outline of a survey that enables you to gather information about how to best service your teachers.

_____

_____

_____

_____

_____

_____

_____

_____

_____

_____

_____

_____

_____

_____

_____

How do I help teachers set goals?

Last school year, I worked with a coaching pair. This was the first time I had virtually coached two coaches from the same school. I spoke with the coaches to talk about their experiences in helping teachers set goals. One of their biggest struggles was to get teachers to set goals that were intentional and could be justified by data.

Before I met with the coaches, I had them complete a survey about their biggest struggle. This helped me understand where they were in helping teachers.

Here is one of the coaches' response:

> My co-coach and I have a running joke that if we hear a teacher say the phrase "I feel like . . ." in one more meeting, that we may snap. We are both new coaches to this school, and we are blazing the trail in implementing data analysis and PLC as a regular part of the school week in a school culture that previously have not valued these things. When asking teachers about their student achievement goals, or their professional growth goals for themselves, we often hear, "Well, I feel like I could get better at teaching writing" "I feel like my class has poor problem solving skills" "I feel like this student may need to be Tier II." It has become a routine that when one of us is in a meeting, a teacher would talk about how they feel about the situation, and when we ask to see data that supported it our teachers become very frustrated.

In coaching we frequently get this kind of reaction. Many teachers set goals or create goals based on what they think should happen instead of really reflecting on the data and being very intentional about what they improve. Sometimes, it's like "shoot for the moon and land among the stars." This could be good in some situations, but in most situations, it's best to make a goal with great intention based on what the students' needs are.

Regarding the situation with my coaches, I am not saying that a teacher's instincts don't count. Believe me, I know we have teacher instincts. In my time in the classroom, I had multiple gut feelings about something. What I did with those feelings, however, was follow them through with observing and collecting evidence. For example, I once suspected that a child couldn't see my whiteboard based on the way she was copying her homework in her agenda. She was a fifth grader with an advanced reading level, but her homework was always written in phonetic spelling. I moved her seat much closer to the board and made a point to look at her writing every day for a week. When I saw the drastic difference, I called her mom and cited specific dates that I had noticed the problem, and the steps I took to help, along with the results. The student was taken to the eye doctor the following week and was prescribed glasses. Notice how I didn't email her mom the first time I noticed the strange spelling and say, "I feel like your daughter can't see," or "Your daughter's spelling does not reflect her reading level. I feel like she's dyslexic." As a mother, my first questions in response to either of those claims would be: Why do you think that? and What evidence do you have to support it? I had to collect the evidence and make a decision based on the collection of evidence. I could have easily and immediately completed the paperwork to refer her to Tier II and asked for additional support, but I didn't have all the evidence just yet to support it. So how could I have created a goal for that student?

During the time I worked with those two coaches, we discovered that the data did not support the teachers' feelings, but by looking at the data, we found other issues. Some students did not need to be Tier II; some of their test data was in the 80th percentile or higher, but some students who had not been identified were now on the radar.

As coaches, we have to be careful not to let our teachers set goals this way. Teachers' hunches are sometimes grounded in bias against a student, whether they realize it or not. One student may be a little hyperactive and reminds a teacher so much of a former student who had impulse-control issues and was later recommended for the SPED program. The teacher's biases can cause her to believe that the student must need Tier II services, when really the student is fine academically. The student is not finishing his work on time, but is not struggling either. The teacher's frustration with the student should be acknowledged, and strategies should be offered to help, but you have to focus Tier II efforts on the students who truly need them. Teachers and coaches need to look at evidence first when setting goals and go from there. If you have teachers who feel strongly about something, but no evidence is collected, help the teachers set up a system for collecting it. They feel like their class is weak in problem solving? Create a spreadsheet for each math test, and log the percentage of computation problems the children got correct, versus the application problems. Chances are that the teachers are right, but it is also possible that they've given two tough math tests in a row and are forgetting how well the past chapters went. Maybe they need more time to teach the content.

Coaching Thought

Goal setting is as simple as looking at the data, finding the need, and creating an action plan based on that need. The goal should be measurable, and it's even better if you can create checkpoints along the way. If the teacher wants 95 percent of her students to score a 3 or higher on the state's writing test at the end of the year, figure out what the first step toward achieving that goal is. Do the students need to write one solid paragraph based on a prompt? Do they need to be able to write a solid paragraph about whatever they choose? Collect some writing samples, analyze the status of the class, and how far they have to go to meet the state's criteria for a "3. Break down the list of skills they need into benchmarks. The teacher can work on reading a passage and pulling out evidence to respond to a question for a couple of weeks, then move on to drafting an outline using that evidence. Whatever the goals may be, the teacher should be actively pursuing information about where her class is on the road toward meeting them.

How will you help teachers set goals? How often will you set the goals? Will you have the teachers complete a "feel/discovery" questionnaire prior to your goal-setting meeting? What data will you have teachers use to support their goals? How will you monitor those goals? These are the questions you need to sit and think about before your school year starts. Spending time answering these questions will give you some idea about how you want to help teachers set goals. Each building and culture is different, and you want to think about your building and experiences in particular when developing your plan of action.

_____

_____

_____

_____

_____

_____

_____

_____

_____

_____

_____

_____

_____

_____

What suggestions do you have when giving constructive criticism to new teachers?

Providing feedback is tough! Why? Because many people are not open to hearing about things that they need to improve on. Let's keep it all the way real! How many times have you gotten feedback from a principal or a coach and immediately thought, "He has no idea what he is talking about. He has never taught third grade." "She was in the classroom for only three years, and I've been in the classroom for twelve, and she has no idea what she is talking about." "I wonder, can he do that with the group of students I am teaching?" I know I have challenged feedback before on so many levels, so I am not saying that this is going to be easy, but it will be necessary.

First, you need to use a cautious approach when giving criticism, and be sure it is constructive so that you build positive relationships with teachers. Don't go blazing into a classroom and start handing out advice without justification. Remember the coach I mentioned earlier in the book? The one who forced her way into classrooms to observe and give feedback? How the notes she wrote fueled the teachers' fire? I have observed teaching teams who ate lunch together every day and saw how they went around sharing the remarks on the notes the principal and coach left for them, all the while rolling their eyes and scoffing at the remarks. Not because the remarks weren't good stuff; they very well may have been. It was because of the way the messages were delivered. If your principal asks you to go into a classroom, have a conversation with the teacher first, and find when she wants you to visit her classroom. That way, you are invited, and your words of wisdom will be less likely to fall on deaf ears.

Second, when you are in the act of delivering feedback to a teacher, be sure to keep it focused on your common goal: the students. Constructive feedback is supportive feedback, and it should help teachers identify solutions to the areas they need to work on. The feedback must be delivered with positive intentions and address specific issues or concerns. If a teacher is weak or needs improvement in one or two areas, that doesn't mean he is an entirely weak teacher, and he should not be left with that impression. Your goal is to give constructive feedback that the teacher can use to improve or make corrections. It should definitely enhance a teacher's toolbox.

Third, be aware of the differences between giving teachers constructive feedback, which is empowering, and destructive feedback, which is attacking. Many times, we give teachers feedback that focuses on what they are doing wrong and that points out all their faults, but we don't follow up with suggestions on how to improve. Destructive feedback offers no practical advice or support suggestions.

Finally, here are four things to consider when providing constructive feedback:

1. Focus on what you observed and what actually happened in the classroom. Use your video observations, your scripts, or your observation form notes as a way to collect the data needed to help teachers improve. Do not infer what happened or what could have happened. It is important to use actual data.

2. Focus on the behavior of the teachers and students and not on the actual person. You will have better relationships with certain teachers because we gravitate to certain people more than others, and that is fine. But do not allow your personal likes or biases to interfere with your ability to provide feedback on what happened in the classroom.

3. Focus on things that can be changed in the classroom rather than things that are beyond our control. If you go into a classroom and observe something of that can't be changed, there is no point in providing feedback if you or the teacher have no way to change to it. Yes, you can acknowledge that it is a problem, but begin by addressing issues and solutions for things that can be immediately changed and have the greatest impact.

4. Be sure to provide specific recommendations and examples of solutions that teachers can put to use. If you point out an issue in a classroom that needs to be improved upon, always have an example of how the teacher can improve the situation. Although you want to be sensitive to whether a teacher thinks she can make an improvement, it's always best to make a suggestion, perhaps play a video showing the suggestion being implemented or an article on how the strategy is implemented so that you can have a discussion around the suggestion.

Coaching Thought

Your role is not to fix teachers or to show them how to teach. You are there to make sure the students grow, which is what the teachers want, too! Hopefully, they know your intentions through the beginning of the year introductions but that you are there to coach and challenge them to do better. You are not there to gloss over their areas of need and spread sunshine and rainbows everywhere. You are there to make them better so that the students can be better. Keep the conversation student-focused, data-driven, and free from as many subjective statements about their teaching as you can, but do not skip the hard stuff.

Write your thoughts on providing constructive feedback and challenges you believe you need to overcome.

_____

_____

_____

_____

_____

_____

_____

_____

_____

_____

_____

_____

_____

What are some communication strategies I can use as a coach?

You and I have been in education long enough to know that every building has an issue with communication. Walk into any school building in the country and ask teachers about the communication of their building, and you will get one of two answers. There is too much communication, or there is not enough communication. Thus, as you begin a school year, know that the way you communicate will play a large part in the way people open up to you. I have found that I will never satisfy everyone's expectations around communication, so I now focus on creating different outlets and utilizing strategies with my interpersonal communication skills. Interpersonal communication is simply two or more people sharing thoughts or feelings with one another. In our role as instructional coaches, we tend to communicate in four specific ways: face-to-face, nonverbal, written, and orally.

Face-to-face communication: As often as possible, try to stick with face-to-face meetings. When starting out as a new coach in a building or even when changing your role in the same building, these meetings are especially important. Having such meetings with teachers allows you to build and create trusting relationships. I highly suggest hosting all feedback conversations and goal-setting meetings in a face-to-face setting. Why? Because other forms of communication can be misconstrued. You want to be able to deliver that information with clarity and give teachers the opportunity to ask you directly clarifying questions, and not in the company of others. Many times in my coaching the coach programs, coaches have sent emails with constructive feedback, with no face-to-face conversation about the feedback, and the teachers have taken things the wrong way. They shared the emails with other teachers and asked their opinions, and what was a simple constructive idea to make things better turned into an outright war. Being open and honest is good, but you must know how to present the information as well. Doing so in a supportive tone in a face-to-face meeting is the best way to provide feedback to teachers; it is also appropriate for teachers who have knocked the ball out of the park, and you want to give them accolades. Do it in person and then always follow up with an email.

Nonverbal communication: Imagine that you are standing at the door of a room and looking through the window at a group of teachers during a staff meeting. Just by observing everyone's posture, facial expressions, and actions, you immediately know that this is indeed a boring staff meeting. This is what we call nonverbal communication. Your posture, facial expressions, and body movements reflect your thoughts and signal them to others. As coaches, we need to pay attention to our body language as well as the body language of others. When you have a face-to-face meeting with a teacher, be aware of how you are delivering information. The tone of your voice is important (we will get into that later), but also the "tone" of your body language is important. You want to convey a sense of support, not that the teacher is in trouble or is doing something wrong. Even if she is, you can present your message in such a way that the teacher understands. If your body language is off and the teachers feels that you are not supportive, whatever you say with have no relevance. The teacher will pick up on the negative body language and become defensive. In addition, when you are delivering feedback, teachers will convey their body language, and you should be able to "read" whether or not they understand you or if they are uncomfortable. If you sense the latter, you can change the tone of the meeting and help the teacher relax, which will give you a chance to better explain your feedback. Here's another example: You are teaching a lesson and checking for understanding, and when you ask CFU questions, students are not answering them correctly. You skim the room and see that the students are not understanding just by their reactions. Some look confused, and some student's heads are turned down. Some students lean back, and some have even started doodling. In that moment of observation, you quickly think of a different way to explain the concept so that the students understand what you are saying. Giving feedback is no different. Reading nonverbal cues are important and giving supportive nonverbal cues are even more important.

After a year of coaching meetings with teachers, I learned to make mental notes of what body language cues I needed to work on. Here are a few of the notes I made for myself.

When I am in a meeting with my teachers, I try to sit up straight and make eye contact so that the teachers know I am paying very close attention to what they have to say. I am aware that in some cultures eye contact can be perceived as disrespectful, so make sure you are culturally sensitive when making this decision. It has worked for me thus far.

I always place my arms and hands on the table. I know this may seem insignificant, but it lets teachers know that I am not on my phone and that I am giving them my full attention. This posture may at first make teachers nervous, but as the conversation goes on, they tend to become very comfortable and relaxed.

I never place my chin in my hand. This tells the teacher or any person you are talking to that you are bored. Actually, someone had to point this out to me. I could be paying very close attention, but my chin in my hand apparently causes me to have a bored look on my face.

I tend to take notes when I am discussing how a lesson is going. I do have the notes where the teacher can see what I am writing or typing. However, if the relationship has not been built, the teacher may feel as though I am writing something that can be used against them. Knowing this writing where they can see has helped me build that trust and relationship.

Written communication: One way in which we as coaches document our work, our follow-up, and our appointments and transmit what's happening is through written communication. Written communication includes emails, weekly newsletters, positive feedback cards, walkthrough forms, coaching plans, and so on. Written communication seems to be the most utilized method of communication, but it's not always the most effective. It does allow you to refer back to what was said, it serves as a reminder to what needs to be done, and it documents your thoughts and actions. Although all types of communication have dos and don'ts, with written words things can be a bit tricky. Why? Because the written word is left to the interpretation and perception of the person reading it.

The tone of an email is expressed by your word choice, your punctuation, whether you use lowercase or uppercase letters, the syntax of sentences, sentence length, your greeting, and your closing. So here are a few dos and don'ts I have learned along the way.

Dos

I start all of my coaching emails by saying "Greetings" followed by the person's last name, for example, "Greetings Ms. Turner." This sets a professional tone to the email. I find that even if I have a personal relationship with a teacher, this allows the communication to stay on a professional level.

I always end with "Educationally" again; this closes the email professionally, and it also reminds the recipient that it's all education and my work in the field.

I sit and think about the words that I am using in an email, especially when it's a follow-up to a verbal conversation with a teacher. I make sure I am not attacking the teacher, and I send the email as a clarification of our conversation to make sure I had the intended takeaways.

Don'ts

In my emails, I do not use all uppercase letters, boldface, or underlines unless there's a deadline. This is important because I never want teachers to think I am yelling at them. Usually, uppercase letters mean you are screaming, and professionals don't screams at each other.

I never use the exclamation point after a sentence more than once. I am sure you have seen this in emails and text, "Please don't go that way !!!!!!" This is meant to highly emphasize the message, but can send the wrong message in a professional setting.

I never use text abbreviations or acronyms in a professional email. While the sender may understand what they mean, doing so is not appropriate in the workplace.

<u>Oral communication:</u> As with written communication, it is important to be aware of your voice tone and word choice during your delivery. Oral communication is a powerful tool. You can motivate, inspire, encourage, cheer up, teach, make sad, tear down someone's motivation, build them up, and even change their mood. So when you are speaking with a colleague, it is important to orally communicate with confidence using a supportive tone. I have learned to be a listener first, repeat what I hear for clarification, and then respond. This has allowed me to communicate effectively and to take time to digest what someone is saying before I respond. I am able to clarify what is asked of me and then respond with the correct calm and direct answer even in a hostile environment. Would you believe that I have had teachers and administrators yell and scream at me? But it was because of my calm verbal responses that I was able to deescalate the situation and turn things around. Keep your cool, watch your tone and words, and be cautious of what you say to teachers. It can build or destroy your relationship building.

As an instructional coach, you may have the opportunity to communicate before large groups at staff meetings, or maybe even at a district-wide professional development session. If so, always present yourself as being confident about what you are saying, but smile often so that teachers know you are approachable. I was working with a coach, and during our first coaching session, she told me about her first coaching experience. She said that she'd had absolutely no idea what she was doing or what the year would hold for her. On the first day back for teachers, the principal asked her to stand up at the staff meeting and share a little about what her job was and how she planned to serve as a resource that year. She spoke of remembering her feelings of dizziness as she walked to the front of the staff meeting that day, but she maintained calm, gave eye contact, spoke clearly, and smiled often. Near the end of the year, a teacher emailed her saying that he had thought of her as their personal mentor that year, and knew from that first staff meeting that she was the right kind of person to help them grow, because she was so confident in what she believed. As she told me that story, she continued to express how scared out of her mind she was that day. I spoke with her about the way in which she presented and communicated that day and how even if you don't feel confident, using your communication skills will help to build relationships.

Coaching Thought

Communication is a mixture of the above factors, and all are important during your years as a professional. No matter how strongly you feel about being an agent of change, you will not make the impact you want to if you are cold, harsh, or come across as judgmental. Knowing coaches' best communication strategies is a good place to start!

Identify the type of communication at which you are the strongest and why. Identify the type of communication at which you are the weakest and why. Develop a quick plan on how to work on your communication weaknesses.

_____

_____

_____

_____

_____

_____

_____

_____

_____

_____

_____

_____

_____

_____

_____

_____

What are some coaching strategies I can use with my teachers?

As an instructional coach, I'm sure you have heard about several strategies that will help make you an effective and impactful instructional coach. While there are millions of strategies out there, here is a list of strategies that I deem to be the top 10 instructional coach strategies. These are all strategies that I have utilized as an instructional coach within my school district with my teachers and when I worked at the State Department of Education.

Strategy #1 Observations: I know you may not see this as a strategy, but it truly is. Observing is a strategy used to gain an understanding as to what is happening in the classroom and from their set goals based on what we see. After we have set these goals and collected initial data, we use the same observation strategy to collect more data to see if there has been an improvement. From our observations, we create a data log that we can use to show teachers what they are doing well and what they may need to work on a little more.

Strategy #2 Modeling: When you are modeling, you are implementing a technique that you have proposed to the teacher you are instructing. This strategy can be a struggle for most coaches. Modeling can be performed in several different ways. I discussed this earlier in the book and revealed that modeling can be a weak spot for me, so I use an alternative version of the strategy. You can use the modeling strategy in the form of a video showing someone else implementing the strategy, you can get up in front of the teacher's classroom and teach a skill using the process, or you can model for the teacher in the form of role playing. Each method is appropriate because it will show teachers that the strategy can be done, and if they are struggling with the skill, it teaches them how to better utilize a tool you have discussed. I can't stress enough the importance of this strategy.

Strategy #3 Co-teaching: When co-teaching, you are working with the same students your teacher is working with every day. You and the teacher work on the lesson that will be implemented. You both choose parts of the lesson to implement. This strategy is especially good for when you are working with resistant teachers. By getting up and teaching with them, you can show them that their students can benefit from this type of instruction. When you co-teach, you are implementing the ideas that you are trying to "sell" to your teacher, and therefore you are modeling for the teacher at the same time.

Strategy #4 Co-planning: If you utilize the strategy of co-teaching with a teacher, you will want to co-plan with her. These two strategies go hand and hand. Co-planning is when you and the teacher sit down and create a lesson plan together. While you are creating this lesson plan, you can ask the teacher how she will implement the strategies you have discussed in the past. This also gives you a chance to ask her to model what she will do and explicitly say what this will look like when she is teaching.

Strategy #5 Effective feedback: I'm sure you didn't think I would leave this one out! While observing, modeling, co-teaching, and co-planning are great, they are all for nothing if you don't give your teachers effective feedback. When you are giving effective feedback, you are going back and talking to your teachers about what you observed. We spoke about the two types of effective feedback in the previous question. In addition to giving feedback on the walkthrough, you can also take this time to look at the data and discuss whether there is growth or not. Having positive, effective feedback is essential to good coaching moving forward (finding new goals) and your coach–teacher relationship. I'm not saying you have to be sunshine and rainbows, but you do want to make sure your feedback is constructive and not destructive as well.

Strategy #6 Real-time coaching: The real-time coaching strategy is perfect if you have a teacher who is really struggling to grasp a concept or a teacher who is flat out defiant. (I really dislike using this word because we are all professionals, but what else can you call someone who just will not do what needs to be done for the kids? And we say kids who blatantly refuse to do something are defiant all the time! Okay, I am off my soapbox.) When you are using real-time coaching, you are in the room giving the teacher step-by-step instructions as to what to do next as it is happening in real time. Let me be clear, you and the teacher have already discussed the strategy that is being implemented, and the teacher has agreed to follow along. Together, you may have practiced the strategy in role playing and even watched a video on how it will be implemented. Please don't just show up at the teacher's classroom and start real-time coaching. He may not be as receptive, and the kids may be quite confused as to what is happening, so here are a couple of ways you can do this.

The first way is to have a whiteboard and write the next step and show it to the teacher discreetly. Sometimes, I stand in the back of the room or in a corner where students are not really paying attention. I try to be as invisible as possible.

The second way is to stand by the teacher and tell her what to do as the class progresses. Most of the time, I am just whispering in the teacher's ear. In between steps, I walk around and observe students to make sure they are getting the concepts being taught and to see if this instructional or behavioral strategy is effective. Walking around makes you visible, but it's not weird to the students when you are talking with the teacher and she is telling them what to do next. Based on your observations, you tell the teacher what needs to happen next.

I use this strategy more with new teachers who are struggling with classroom management issues. (Not to say that you can't use it for instructional strategies; it just seems to work really well with classroom management strategies.) It's easier to tell the teacher what to next in real time to see that it works. It also allows the teacher to continue to keep the "power" in the classroom. With some groups of students, it's best this way. When I model a behavior strategy, the students may conform, but if the classroom teacher implements the strategy (especially if the teacher has lost control of the class), students may not conform. So I allow the teacher to implement the strategy first. I watch and give her feedback right then so that the students relate the authority to the teacher.

Strategy #7 Data-driven coaching: Every coach should be a data-driven coach. Using data to create or implement instructional strategies is important because we must have something to back up our ideas. We need to have tangible proof that the strategy is necessary. Some districts have data coaches, and that is their only job—to break down the data. They grab data from the district and building levels and review and analyze data from demographics to perceptions to testing, and even data from the staff. True data coaches are usually not involved with the process of instruction.

If you have a data coach in your district, he should work with you to look at the data and pinpoint the areas of weakness. If you don't have a data coach, usually the principal sits with you to review the data. Not all the data that come into the building are for your use.

Instructional coaches use two types of data: assessment/achievement data and implementation/process data.

Assessment/achievement data comes from a recent common assessment such as a district or school-wide benchmark, weekly assessments on a particular skill, or end of a course or chapter test that you as well as the teachers have collected.

Implementation/process data comes from walkthroughs and baseline observations.

Having these types of data allows you to ask questions such as, "Are you seeing growth, or are you seeing the same issues over and over again?" Data from the assessments and observations also allow teachers to be reflective in their practice. It also allows you, as the instructional coach, to have cold hard facts in hand, it makes it easier to either praise or have a difficult conversation with your teacher.

Strategy #8 Video coaching, Part 1: Video coaching is by far my favorite strategy. It allows for concrete evidence-based coaching. There are two ways to look at video coaching, and I have broken them down into strategy number 8 and strategy number 9.

Let's look at strategy number 8.

The first way to implement video coaching is through the use of PLC videos. When you use a PLC video, you will be giving effective feedback after an observation. There are two ways to use the video. The first way to use it is to talk about the strategy you (or hopefully your teacher) has come up with. Then as you watch the video, you pause every so often to ask the teacher probing questions about the strategy.

Stopping the video works best if you have a teacher who is a little reluctant to your ideas. You may want to stop more with such teachers to keep them focused on the task at hand, and to keep "an attitude" out of the way. The second way to implement this strategy is to watch the video all the way through and then discuss it. Either way you use this strategy, make sure you ask probing questions at the end and discuss whether the teacher is willing to try to implement the ideas.

Strategy #9 Video coaching, Part 2: The second part of video coaching actually puts the teacher in front of the camera. You can also do this two different ways.

The first way is to tell the teacher you are going to be recording him. (This is just common courtesy. Also, before using this strategy, clear it with your administration and union rep if you are in a union school. I have worked with coaches where this was not allowed per contract.) When the teacher is being recorded, he will most likely put on his "A-game." If this happens, do not worry about it. There are still flaws in a "perfect" day of instruction, and you will be able to identify areas in which the teacher can use some help. After you record the teacher, you will sit down with him and watch the video. During this time, the teacher will fill out an observation sheet just as you will. Then you begin discussing what you both saw and what you both thought.

The second way to utilize this style of video-coaching is to have the teacher record themselves and send it to you. You watch the video separately and write down notes and feedback. You have the teacher watch his/herself on the video and complete the same form you did. You meet together and watch the video and discuss your reflection sheets.

I use this more than the first way. It is helpful for the teacher to watch themselves alone and absorb the lesson, critique their teaching and then sit down and discuss. I have found that teachers are much more receptive to feedback this way. Then you can help coach across the miles. I do this with two teachers currently and they upload everything to Google Drive, and then I give them feedback.

Strategy #10 Peer-coach-peer observations: Use this strategy when you have a teacher who is not receptive to your feedback, but may be receptive to another co-worker's. There are two ways to use this strategy.

The first way is to have a teacher who is implementing the same or a similar strategy go into the reluctant teacher's classroom and observe. The teacher will write what they observed on an observation form that has been provided for them. Then you and the observing teacher will meet, just the two of you, and then as a group of three later on.

Another way you can use this type of observation is for you and the observing teacher to be in the room together, both observing. The aftermath works about the same. You and the other teacher will discuss what you saw, and then you will bring in the reluctant teacher with the hope the reluctant teacher is more receptive.

Coaching Thought

There are so many strategies out there to help you improve your coaching. Above is just a small list of strategies I have successfully implemented throughout my coaching career. Remember, whatever strategies you use, you want to build positive relationships in the classroom. A reluctant teacher can turn over a new leaf with a little respect, and a whole lot of patience.

Choose a coaching strategy that you have never used but want to try. Think of a teacher who could benefit from the use of this strategy. Plan out how you will use this strategy with that teacher. How will you approach this teacher to use the new strategy? How will you reflect? How will you perfect?

_____

_____

_____

_____

_____

_____

_____

_____

_____

_____

_____

_____

_____

_____

_____

_____

_____

What are the "musts" for the beginning of the year to help support teachers, and what planning is needed?

One of the first things you can tackle at the beginning of the year (even before you have your caseload) is to get your space set up. Take a look around because this will be your home base! What do you have to work with? Do you have an office? Are you equipped with space large enough to meet with teachers? Do you have a space that could allow you to teach teachers? I have been in closet spaces, had full classrooms, shared a space with another coach, and even had an office on a rolling cart. So I am here to tell you that you can make anything you've got work; you just have to think creatively.

When you have analyzed the amount of room you have in your space, decide how it will best meet your needs. A great way to do this is to create a rough map of your space and what you picture can be accomplished in each area. There are some things that are nonnegotiable, whether you have a classroom space or a tiny office. Here are a few I always consider when I am creating my space.

Functional workspace: We all know that coaches don't spend much time at their workspace, but when you are there, you want to be sure that you have what you need. Don't put yourself in an area that is awkward to reach, far from outlets, or too small for spreading out papers and your computer at the same time. Picture some of the tasks you will need to accomplish at your workspace (writing up observations, doing documentation, correspondence, and so on, and think about how much space you need for each. Make sure you have it!

Storage for your materials: You will have your own professional development materials, PD materials for the teachers you are coaching, and you might also have student resource materials that are all meant to be stored in your space. Think about keeping the flow of the room intact while also making sure the resources are easily accessible for both you and your teachers.

Wall space: You can really set the tone of your space with what you have on the walls. Consider motivational, instructional, or informational material that can be valuable for those learning in your space and for those stopping by for a quick question. Have fun with it! We've all been in that boring room for meetings—don't make that your room.

Collaboration: If you have a large office or a classroom, create a space that is ideal for working with teachers. Tables with space for multiple teachers as well as a setup that allows for community learning as well as direct instruction will serve you well. Again, picture how an ideal workshop would go and what your setup would be like, and create a space that is conducive to that environment.

Walking into your space for the first time can feel overwhelming. Take your planning in small bites; picture what you want to happen in your space, and then do what you can to create an area where your ideals can be reached.

If you are brand new to your building, but coaches before you have established a great coaching area, take an inventory of the different types of resources you have ready and available in your building. When you meet teachers for planning, you will want to be able to quickly offer resources, lesson materials, plans, and so on, that they can seamlessly bring into their rooms to work toward meeting their goals. Match those resources with your professional library as well. I have used my personal library of books and resources for teachers during my coaching. My personal books are correctly labeled that they belong to me. Only one time have I had an issue with getting a resource returned. I now label each book with a black sharpie with my last name on the outside.

If you have money to spend, look at the gaps in your resources. Maybe the school building has had different initiatives throughout the years, and the way resources have been purchased shows it. There may be eight different phonics series, because there was a huge phonics push for a few years, but there is little to support upper grades with writing. Chances are, if the school has not prioritized something in the past, teachers may feel a little uneasy in that area, and you may be getting quite a few requests to work in that area, and you will also see a huge deficiency in that area and need to provide help there. You may as well have a few books to share right from the beginning.

Another "must" is a general familiarity with the content your teachers are responsible for, and what is developmentally appropriate for different grade levels. I have found that creating a resource binder that includes the state-required standards for each grade level or subject I support has been a lifesaver for me. I often pull this binder out during my one-on-one meetings with teachers and even reference it when preparing for my debrief conversations. If you were lucky enough to be hired in your position before the summer break, then spend some time in the summer reading the standards and breaking them down. Become very familiar with them so that, as you are observing, you will have a basic sense of what you should expect in a room, if best practices are being observed.

Take some time to meet with your principal. It is crucial that you know exactly what the principal's vision is for the building before you get too carried away with your own goals. Many ideas that coaches have for their buildings fail during their first year as a coach because they didn't understand from the beginning that the principal did not value the same things that they valued. I have learned through my many experiences throughout the years that I am a helper in delivering the vision rather than the creator of the vision of the building. The principal is steering the car, and you are going to get frustrated quickly if you are sitting in the backseat yelling directions to where you think you are going, but his GPS is taking him somewhere else.

During your meeting, it is a good idea to ask questions to help you determine if you are on the same page before you begin.
Some great ones to start with may be:

> What are your goals for this school year?
> What do you value about your staff?
> What do you look for when you walk through a teacher's room?
> What do you envision your role being in your building?

Now that you have the resources you need or have created a list of resources and met with your principal, one of the most important musts at the beginning of the year is to plan the first meetings with teachers. By now, you should know the number of teachers you will be supporting. If you are a coach whose model of support is the teacher volunteer model, I suggest setting up a one-on-one meeting with as many teachers as possible.

Think about the beginning of the school year schedule and what's happening in the first few weeks of school. Choose a week, I prefer week two, in which you can meet with all your teachers, although the meetings may have to extend into the next week. I always choose week two because, during the first week, classroom teachers' time is filled with getting to know the students, learning routines and procedures, possibly doing assessments, and on and on. To be honest, they don't have time for me that first week! A better use of my time during the first week that students are in school is to see if I can support any of my teachers as they get started. In my recent years, I have supported the front office staff and even the guidance department in the high school. That said, you do want to be sure that you are meeting with your teachers by the end of week two so that you are ready to start your coaching cycles by week three!

As you begin to plan to meet with your teachers, try to think about using a theme for your first meetings. This helps create a sense of community and makes for a more relaxed setting, but you still need to be all about the business. One theme I have used several times that has been well received is "Cupcakes with Coach." To host this theme, I purchased several types of cupcakes, water, coffee, tea, and hot chocolate for teachers to snack on and drink during our meeting. This allowed the teachers to know that I cared about them and that I was doing something special just for them. It also set a relaxed tone for the meeting. Choose a theme that makes sense for your building.

After you have your theme, you need to set the agenda for the meeting. It is important to know that this meeting should be forty-five minutes at a maximum. You don't want to overwhelm your teachers at the first meeting. Thirty to forty-five minutes is plenty of time to get a sense of each teacher and pass along necessary information.

Here is a sample agenda that I use each year and what each item should include:

Introduction
>A quick get to know you! How long have you been teaching, what grades, how long in this building, and so on?

Gather background information
>Ask questions! How do the teachers feel about coaching? Did they want to participate with a coach, or did someone require them too? What general issues are they having in their classroom?

Define your coaching and teacher roles
>Getting yourselves on the same page and setting norms at this point is huge. I find that it's vital to set norms with your teachers early on. At the end of each meeting, decide together what actions you will work on and prioritize following through.

Set goals
>What do the teachers want to work on? What are their goals? If you have done a baseline observation, you will use that at this point as well.

Review coaching cycles
>Share the cycle with them. Some may already know, but some may not. Be sure they all leave with an understanding of what your coaching cycles will look like.

Go over baseline observation if applicable

Discuss important dates (e.g., testing, upcoming deadlines, etc.)
>Make sure you know what they have on their upcoming schedules, and make sure they know if you will need anything from them in the near future. Communication is key here.

Schedule your first or second observation
>If you have already done a baseline observation, go ahead and schedule your second one. If you haven't, let them know that you'll be coming through in the near future to observe them.

Go over next steps
>If you've already done your first observation, you should have set goals and be off and running in your coaching cycle. Take this time to make sure the goals are clear and set a date for your second observation. If you haven't done the initial observation yet, take this time to set a date to get that done.

Coaching Thought

You've made it! You've landed the job or signed on for another year. After you let out a sigh of relief that hurdle is passed, it's time to get prepared for the year ahead. Starting the year off prepared sets the tone for the rest of the school year. So make sure you take some time to complete the preceding tasks even if you have a late start.

Beginning of Year Checklist:

> Analyze your space.
>
> Map out your space.
>
> Organize your space.
>
> Set up your coaching system.
>
> Plan your first meeting with teachers.
>
> Carry out your first meeting with teachers.
>
> Plan your first observation.
>
> Conduct your first observations

Take some time to focus on the above-mentioned tasks. Check out your space, take a quick inventory, label your materials, set up a meeting with your principal, and create and the theme and agenda for your first meeting with teachers. Write a few ideas for each and set a timeline and date to complete each task. In addition, I have created a quick checklist for the beginning of the year. Each one of these steps are addressed in this book.

_____

_____

_____

_____

_____

_____

_____

_____

_____

_____

_____

_____

_____

_____

_____

_____

_____

_____

Part IV

Utilizing Coaching Cycles

"Coaching is about helping you think more deeply about your work, organize your thoughts, set your own goals, and develop a plan to meet those goals"

- Nina Morel

What is an instructional coaching cycle?

In your role as an instructional coach, you will be expected to conduct and track your work using instructional coaching cycles. An instructional coaching cycle is just a different way of providing professional development. Instead of providing professional development in a whole class setting, you work in partnership with a teacher to improve his instruction or classroom management. It's called a cycle because it involves completing the same steps over and over again as a way to continuously improve an action. You can follow several different cycles, but the basics of every cycle will consist of a first meeting or the goal-setting meeting, an observation and data collection, some type of learning, and a reflection using data. Again, there are many variations. The cycle will be different for each teacher because the starting point will not be the same for every teacher you work with. Based on your observations and your work, you will decide where to begin with a teacher. I discuss this topic in greater depth later in this part of the book.

Coaching Thought

Coaching cycles are the staple of every coaching role. Whether you coach instruction, behavior, or technology, you must use a coaching cycle.

Research or ask your district which coaching cycle method they prefer you use. If they do not have a preference, utilize the question, "What are the components of an instructional coaching cycle and how do I use them?" to develop a model cycle for yourself.

_____
_____
_____
_____
_____
_____
_____
_____
_____
_____
_____
_____
_____
_____
_____

What is the purpose of the instructional coaching cycle?

The main purpose of the instructional coaching cycle is to improve an action by building a teacher's capacity in the area in which you are working. Moreover, an instructional coaching cycle instills structure and consistency in your coaching with teachers. It enables you to track improvement and collect data that you can use to reflect on your work.

Coaching Thought

Adhering to an instructional coaching cycle will allow you to track your work as an instructional coach and be a powerful tool for teacher and student improvement.

In your own words, write why you think it's important to use an instructional coaching cycle in your work.

_____

_____

_____

_____

_____

_____

_____

_____

_____

_____

_____

_____

_____

_____

What are the components of an instructional coaching cycle and how do I use them?

An instructional coaching cycle has a before, during, and after period in which certain meetings take place. Think of it the same way you think of teaching a new unit to students. Before you begin, you try to get a sense of how much of the unit they already know and what their comfort level is with the material. This may be garnered through a pretest, watching them perform certain skills, checking entrance slips, and so on. During the unit, you plan according to your preliminary data, making sure you meet all the learning needs in your room. After you provide all the knowledge you can, while monitoring the students' learning as you taught, you give some sort of post-assessment test.

The coaching cycle is very similar. You get a sense for what teachers need help with first, or they may tell you where they want to begin; you coach them through it, finding a way to measure their growth along the way; and then you compare where they began to what they have achieved. You may be coaching toward a big moment: a district screening assessment, a school holiday that you've set as a deadline for meeting a certain goal, and so on. Or you may simply be going through the cycle over and over until a teacher has met his goals.

The actual coaching part can take many forms. Maybe you model a series of lessons and then observe in order to give feedback. Maybe you and your teacher opt to video a series of lessons, and you coach based on what you see in the video. Maybe you plan a series of co-teaching lessons. (I mention several strategies in Part III of the book.) Whatever the case may be, the cyclical nature of coaching stays the same, though your approach may change.

For simplicity, I have divided the coaching cycle into three sections: The "before" meeting, the "during" meeting, and the "after" meeting.

The before meeting: This meeting can consist of the first meeting, a goal-setting meeting, an observation conversation, or a combination of all three. The style of the meeting begins with the type of support a teacher needs.

If you have a teacher who is struggling with classroom management, you will likely need to conduct an observation prior to the meeting so that you can discuss what you saw and to get a feel for what the teacher needs are and where to begin. Most of the time, I know when a teacher is struggling with classroom management because when I stop by to speak or just check in, the class is unruly and evidence of the struggle is written on the teacher's face. In this case, I will stop by and just tell the teacher I will be in sometime that day or the next day to do a quick observation for our coaching cycle meeting. I give a fair warning that I will be coming by. Why? Well, I want the teacher to know I'm coming so that she can prepare herself and is aware that we are going to start a coaching cycle. When I tell teachers this, they usually try their hardest to do everything "right by the book." But if they are giving their best and are still struggling, then I can see exactly how to help them. After my observation, I'm able to prepare for our meeting, and in our meeting, we can discuss the observation and develop a plan and a goal all at once.

If I am working with a teacher and we previously discussed a strategy we are going to implement, during our meeting, we will discuss the strategy, doing some type of modeling (e.g., watching a video of the strategy being implemented, me modeling and showing it, reading a quick article or reviewing a lesson plan about it) and setting a goal for the outcome. We will also create a timeline and set a date for implementation and for me to model or observe the teacher implementing the strategy in the classroom.

If I am working with a teacher who is seeking content planning, my coaching cycle will begin differently. We will email each other a few times to identify the standard and skill the teacher will be teaching. Previous to our meeting, I will pull several different types of resources to discuss, and during the meeting, we will create together a powerful lesson (or lessons) utilizing several resources and strategies. The teacher will implement the resource and strategies, and I will observe.

The during meeting: This can consist of some type of learning, observation, and data collection. After I meet with teachers and we develop a plan, it is time for action. Again, the type of action I take will depend on my coaching focus.

When a teacher is struggling with classroom management, the cycle will be more involved. I tend to use more hands-on coaching strategies, and I'm more present in the classroom. My favorite strategy is to use real-time coaching. During our meeting, we discuss my observations, and we both decide on a plan of action. I will visit the classroom and help the teacher implement the strategy. One rule that I use (some agree and some disagree) is to never model a classroom management strategy in the classroom. Why? Here's my theory: if I model for the class, of course they will listen and fall in line. I'm not the classroom teacher; I'm someone different, and they will listen to me just because they are not pushing my buttons or trying to see what they can get away with. When I was an administrator, I learned that if I went into a classroom and took over, the students respected me and did what I asked them to do while I was there, but when I left and the teacher tried to continue with the same expectation, often the teacher struggled, because we had transferred the power to me. As a coach, I always keep this in mind. I always want teachers to have control over their classrooms, and allowing them to implement a new strategy allows them to do just that.

I show up and always let the teacher give directions and implement the strategy. Real-time coaching consists of two styles (which I explain in Part II). The first time I work with a teacher, I like to be side-by-side with him.

The teacher is in control giving all the directions, and I am walking around the room observing what is happening as the teacher implements the strategy. At some point, I will walk to the teacher and whisper a next step based on the reaction of the students. Because the teacher is in control, the students will not lose respect for him. I am in the background. The students are not acting appropriately because of me or even paying attention to me because I'm just walking around and helping out when I can. So to the student, I look like the teacher's assistant. I continue to give feedback to the teacher during the entire lesson. I can see things the teacher does not because he is actively in the moment, and I am observing.

The next time I visit the classroom, I will utilize a strategy in which I am in the back of the room, prepared to give cues to the teacher for what should happen next. I may walk around the classroom as before so that the students and teacher can feel more relaxed, but I am still guiding the teacher through the implementation process. In between the two real-time sessions, the teacher and I will meet to discuss the first time he implemented the strategy, and we will discuss what went right and what needs help. I also make it a point to discuss students who appear to be big challenges and help develop a proactive plan. If such students improve, then you should do that. This helps manage situations that may arise and catch the teacher off guard. Having these conversations helps the teacher become more comfortable. Real-time coaching may be needed frequently before it is time for the "after" meeting.

You may recall that during the "before" period, the teacher implementing the new teaching strategy and I did some type of modeling, which helped prepare the teacher implement the strategy. What I do in the "during" period is based on the comfort level of the teacher I'm coaching. If the teacher needs me to model and teach, I do that and have the teacher watch and then complete a modeling coaching observation form.

On this form, the teacher has the focus and questions she needs to be looking for as she observes me. We will meet quickly and discuss what she saw and then how she can transfer it into the way she will implement the strategy. The teacher then implements the strategy, and I will observe using the same focus and questions the teacher used. Doing so allows us to compare how I implemented the strategy with how she implemented it.
We will then move to the "after" period.

The teacher who needed help with content planning and I will spend some time observing the implementation of the lesson we built together. I will use a focused form, and during our meeting, we will discuss specific things I will look for during the observation. We will then have the after meeting.

The after meeting: This meeting can consist of discussing and reflecting on data and a meeting with a teacher. During this time, I will meet with the teacher to reflect on the entire observation and action process.

The teacher who needs help on classroom management skills and I will meet after several mini meetings, with me conducting "in the moment" coaching. We will discuss the overall implementation and review the goal we set at the beginning of the cycle. Together, we will decide whether we are ready to move on to a different strategy or continue to work on the same strategy but implement it in a different way.

The teacher who needs help implementing a new strategy, and I will review the observation forms and compare notes and discuss what went well and what did not go well. I will use a different type of example. We will discuss the goal set and establish whether the goal was met. If it was met, we will discuss how the teacher can continue to build on what he has already achieved. If the goal was not met, we will talk about the next steps we need to take and devise a different plan and start a new cycle.

The teacher who needs help in content planning and I will meet to discuss the observation and give feedback on what went well and what needs to be improved. Based on my observation, I will pull resources (e.g., videos, books and/or articles) to give the teacher more support in developing future lessons on the subject. Based on the observation and if the goal is met, we will discuss a future cycle and the nature of the cycle. If the teacher is doing well, I will suggest a video coaching cycle in which the teacher will video tape himself, review the video, complete the video self-observation form, and share the video with me to review. I will pull some specific things out of the video, and we will discuss and watch the video together, thereby bringing both of our observations to the table. The meeting will be primarily a reflection based on the video, a discussion on how things can improve, and identifying the support needed for the next steps.

Coaching Thought

Except for building trust and relationships, learning how to conduct effective coaching cycles is the most challenging task for a coach to navigate. Understanding the components and precisely what to do are essential. Different instructional methods are brought into each coaching cycle. But the core values remain the same— identify the goal, determine the steps to reach the goal, take the steps, reflect and evaluate your success—and these can be divided into before, during, and after periods of time and meetings.

If you are a new coach, how do you see yourself utilizing the coaching cycles? Identify where you will need more support in implementation. If you are a seasoned or experienced coach, reflect on the information. How do you, or can you, include these components in all your coaching cycles? Have you been differentiating your cycles? How will you use this information to better your coaching cycles? Identify the areas in which you need more support.

_____

_____

_____

_____

_____

_____

_____

_____

_____

_____

_____

_____

_____

_____

_____

_____

_____

_____

How can coaching cycles increase effectiveness in my work as an instructional coach?

As I mentioned in the question on the purpose of a coaching cycle, coaches use instructional coaching cycles to keep coaching on track and organized. When considering the effectiveness or success of an instructional coach's work, you look for how the coach was able to be successful. Organization and routines are strategies that highly successful people use. When coaches are coaching multiple teachers, having an organized system to implement and follow creates a routine. Some coaches coach many teachers in separate buildings, and that causes for organization and documentation for their work. In addition, conducting an instructional coaching cycle sets an expectation of what will happen next for both the teacher and coach. It takes the guesswork out of your role with the teacher, and the teacher will be prepared for what happens next.

Coaching Thought

Utilize the coaching cycle to create a routine for your work.

How will you track your coaching cycles? Are you provided with coaching forms to track them? If not, check out the website www.simplycoachingandteaching.com, where you can find forms you can use to track your coaching.

_____

_____

_____

_____

_____

_____

_____

_____

_____

_____

_____

_____

_____

_____

What are strategies for implementing effective coaching cycles?

When I was a new coach, coaching cycles were a struggle for me. I had to discover just how to implement them. I understood the components of the cycles and what went into each part, but I struggled to find a model on implementation. I reached back into my teacher strategy toolbox and realized that I could utilize the gradual release teaching model to implement my coaching cycles. Taking the "I Do, We Do, You Do" model was the perfect way to pull together my cycles. When I was in the classroom, I would gradually allow my students to move from the stage of limited knowledge to taking control of their learning and becoming independent. My role as the teacher moved more toward the role of facilitator of learning rather than the holder of knowledge, and that is just what I do with my teachers.

Allow me to explain. Every coaching cycle has a before, during, and after, and within that model, you meet and set a goal, observe, teach, and reflect. You implement by executing the gradual release. When working with a teacher, you as the coach will observe and meet with the teacher to identify the goal and strategy the teacher will work on. You will then complete an "I Do," which is when you teach something new by modeling it for the teacher or watching a video of the strategy being implemented or even reading a model or excerpt from a book. But the teacher is gaining new knowledge about the strategy to implement, even if it's a strategy she is familiar with. The teacher will implement the strategy with support from you; this is the "We Do" part. The teacher can implement the strategy, and you will support by helping the teacher practice before teaching in front of the classroom. This model allows you to utilize real-time coaching by implementing it to the class and then allowing the teacher to implement the strategy immediately, or use signals or an ear bud radio in the back of the classroom and give immediate feedback as the teacher is implementing the strategy. You are right there helping the teacher along. Now that you have assisted the teacher in implementation, you allow them to implement the strategy alone while you observe in order to collect data, reflect on it, and give feedback. That's the "You Do" part.

In this way, you complete a full coaching cycle. Coaching cycles can be repeated over and over for the same strategy, and you can work on the strategy for a week, a month, or even an entire school year. The difference is that each cycle has a specific goal or small benchmark to help you reach the overall goal. So don't move too quickly to the next benchmark if the teacher hasn't "mastered" the strategy. Just as you had to reteach a skill to students in multiple ways, you may need to do the same with teachers. And it's okay. Teachers can benefit from the same principles. After all, you are still a teacher too. You are now simply a teacher of teachers, but the most effective methods of instruction will still work in this setting.

Not all teachers will need this intensive type of implementation. I usually use this approach when I have a new teacher, a teacher who needs support in behavior or classroom culture management, a teacher who has not yet implemented the strategy, or a teacher you deem needs this support. As a coach, you should be able to detect the type of support each teacher will need based on your observations and your relationship. On the other hand, it may be advisable to use this approach with all your teachers, and then sort out who needs this kind of support, especially if you are new to the building.

Coaching Thought

Be sure you are always a listener and observer. Just as students have different learning styles and need different levels of intervention, so do your teachers.

Rewrite this in your own words for understanding. Doing so will enable you implement and understand how the coaching cycle and implementation works.

_____
_____
_____
_____
_____
_____
_____
_____
_____
_____
_____
_____
_____
_____
_____
_____
_____

How can I have an effective coaching conversation?

Coaching conversations have the power to encourage teachers to continue to improve. In Part III of the book, I discuss providing feedback meetings. In some ways, coaching conversations are just that. You are meeting to provide feedback for an observation. If I am coaching a teacher and we are not at the stage of a feedback meeting, we will have a more generalized coaching conversation. The meeting will still have a flow, and I make sure to include the following:

Praise and connect: I always start the meeting with something positive, even if it is very small. Before the meeting, I intentionally look for something praiseworthy that the class or teacher did. Doing so allows the conversation to start on the right path. Then I try to connect with teachers on a personal level. I might ask, "How are your kids?" or "How is your dog?" or, if the teacher was ill the previous week, "How do you feel today?" I try to ask questions that are meaningful to teachers. I believe doing so helps teachers relax and be open to the upcoming conversation. It also helps build relationships, which is important; otherwise, teachers may think you are "all business" and do not genuinely care about them as individuals.

Establish focus: When you were in the classroom, you began each lesson by announcing or connecting students with the lesson for the day. The same is true when you are coaching teachers. After you complete the usual greetings, you discuss the desired outcomes or the reason for the conversation. If you are meeting about NWEA data, then you might say, "Ms. Turner, during this meeting, we will dig deep into your winter NWEA data results. By the end of our meeting today, we should be able to identify a group of students who need additional instruction with subtracting and regrouping three-digit numbers." At that point, you have stated exactly what you will focus on and what the end result will be. Doing so sets a clear focus on what you will need to accomplish. Often during a meeting, you will get off track, but always bring the conversation back to its established focus.

<u>Be an authentic</u> listener: While hosting coaching conversations, I learned one valuable lesson, listen more, talk less. Someone once told me that I should follow the 90/10 rule. As a coach, it is important that I spend 90 percent of my time listening to the teacher I am coaching and 10 percent of the time talking. During the 90 percent of time that I spend listening, I am able to better understand and serve those I am coaching and what I am coaching. The 10 percent time is spent asking questions to help teachers discover the answers within themselves.

<u>Ask questions with compassion:</u> Having compassion for the teachers you are working with helps to keep you grounded as a teacher first. I have met many coaches and administrators who will question a teacher about her classroom practices, as though they did not understand the classroom situation. Each position in the field of education comes with its own stressors, but making sure you remember what it was like to be a classroom teacher is important. As you ask questions, keep in mind the 90/10 rule mentioned above. That 10 percent should be used to ensure clarity and understanding. But not in a demeaning way. How you say something is much more important than what you say. During my time as an instructional coach, my most challenging principal always gave me very direct feedback. She asked clarifying and probing questions to get me to think and to stretch me beyond my comfort zone. She did it in a way that let me know she believed in my potential.

<u>Plan and discover the next steps:</u> Before you close your conversation with a teacher, be sure to state what the next steps will be. Create a plan together. During the conversation, focus on the outcome and not the obstacles. Write the plan together. This allows both you and the teacher to participate, clarify understanding, and divide the implementation process into manageable steps.

Identify obstacles: After you identify the next steps, fully consider what needs to happen. Some teachers will offer a thousand and one excuses why things can't happen. It is imperative that you do not give them an out. Write about potential roadblocks, the resources needed, and how to get them. I always ask the question, "What might get in the way of you accomplishing your next steps?" Write the answer with your teacher and identify who is responsible for making things happen.

Make the commitment: Ending your conversation with a commitment to achieve the result will help strengthen the possibility of change. I have a really cute commitment sheet that I ask teachers to sign at the end of our meeting. They sign it and I sign it. They take it with them. It is a reminder of what they have committed to do. I write the commitment as a way to follow up, but I don't keep a signed copy because it is not an "I got you." It is a way to help teachers take ownership of their next steps.

Coaching Thought

When having a coaching conversation, remember that the most important objective is the growth of students. If the conversation is student-centered, no one should feel attacked or criticized by your feedback. Keep the conversation as factual as possible so there is little room for misinterpretation. Stick with the data you are collecting and focus on the positive as often as you can, and you will have no trouble taking your teachers far.

Based on the information you have read in Part III and this section, record points that you will include in your coaching conversations.

_____
_____
_____
_____
_____
_____
_____
_____
_____
_____
_____
_____
_____
_____

How does being data-driven fit into my role as a coach?

Being a coach is, or should be, a data-driven profession. Remember that conversations should be as student-centered as possible, and the reason you and the teachers are there is to teach students and ensure their growth. So keeping track of your work as a coach is imperative. You may be in a school that sees data as the holy grail, and you may be the keeper of that data for your building. If that's the case, you probably already know how closely you need to monitor it, analyze it, find areas of improvement, and so on. On the other hand, some schools do not monitor their data methodically. Instead, teachers will keep up with it, if they want to; or keeping and monitoring data may not be encouraged at all. I am still here to tell you that data are important. In your role as a coach, you will use data in three different ways: to track teacher and student data, to host data chats, and to develop data-driven professional development.

When you were a classroom teacher, you saw data as one of your best friends; now as a coach, it can be hard to know exactly what kind of data to track and how much of it you need to track (between teachers and students, you have much to observe). In addition to knowing what to track, it can be difficult to find a way to track your data effectively. One of the top questions the coaches I coach ask is, "How can I ensure I am tracking the right data?"

I track two types of data: teacher data and student data. Each type has its own purpose.

Teacher data: You need to keep track of your teachers' progress, and keep that data in your records, especially if you have the same teachers year after year. When you first meet your teachers, you will set up a goal and the steps that need to happen in order to achieve that goal. After each observation, review the teachers' steps and record the steps they mastered to get closer to achieving the overall goal. Record when the goal was achieved and the evidence showing that it was achieved. You can track this data on a simple teacher–coach goal sheet that you keep with their observation sheets.

Student data: Student-level data is essential to student improvement and to you as an instructional coach. Often your teachers' goals are derived from these data. You can find where students need the most help by examining formative assessments. After you and the teachers identify which assessment you will review, you can look for specific content areas and skills in which students are deficient. Once you identify a focus area, you can work with teachers to develop a pretest and help them find resources to teach the needed skills; then, after a sufficient amount of time, the teachers will be able to give the students a post-test, and you and the teachers can discuss the students' growth.

Between the pretest and the post-test, there should be formal and informal assessments that show whether students are progressing. Since you are working alongside teachers, you will meet and discuss the validity of the assessments and the checks for understanding and anything else the teacher is using. When using formal assessments, your focus is on the students' academic success.

It is important that the data include pretest results, information about growth in between pre- and post-assessments, strategies that are effective, and strategies that aren't effective. Make sure you are tracking all of the physical numbers (the testing data) as well as the strategies and techniques that worked for the students. Tracking the assessment data is good, but the strategies are very important. Why? Because that is how you build a strong teacher. The teacher will understand when to home in on utilizing a particular strategy with his students.

The result is that you must track a lot of data, and using a basic data wall just won't cut it. I have teachers complete a corrective action plan, and I keep it with my observation notes.

Sometimes what you are coaching is not how to teach an academic concept, but are instead coaching a teacher on classroom management, especially new teachers. Whenever people are new to something, it takes them time to get adjusted to it, and you are there to help them adjust. When you decide to set a behavioral goal with a teacher, you follow a similar process as you did with academics. You write the overall goal with the teacher. Next, you find the resources the teacher needs to achieve the goal. Finally, you work with the teacher and observe how the strategies are working in the classroom. You can keep track of the data by noting student behavior and the overall "fluency" of the classroom. If the classroom is running smoothly, the strategies are working.

Tracking data is only one part of your role in the data world. You will have feedback meetings and coaching conversations, but that meaningful conversation is through data chats. Data chats with teachers are exactly what they sound like. They are conversations that you and your teachers have about specific data that you have collected from their classroom. These data chats offer many benefits.

Benefit 1: Data chats help determine essential standards.

As people in education, we all can agree that a number of standards need to be covered throughout the course of a school year. By looking at the data with your teachers, you can figure out which standards you need to emphasize versus those you don't have to push so much.

Such data also gives you a jumping-off place for your goal and reveals where to find the resources your teachers will need to succeed.

<u>Benefit 2: You create an open dialogue with your teacher.</u>

Sometimes teachers are blissfully (or ignorantly) unaware of what the data reveal. In some cases, teachers may try to interpret the data but struggle because it is not their strong suit. Regardless, having an open dialogue with teachers about the data on their classroom is essential, not only for them but also for you.

I'm sure we have all run into the reluctant teacher who doesn't want or "need" our help. In such cases, having data chats is especially important. While reminding your teachers that you are there to help them not tear them down, you can use the data to support your usefulness to their classrooms.

<u>Benefit 3: Data chats give you and your teacher a common goal.</u>

As stated above, data chats can help you come up with a goal for the classroom. Not only does it help create a goal, it can also give you and your teacher a common goal.

Sometimes when we test, teachers already know they haven't hit a certain standard hard enough but have plans to do so. On the flip side, some teachers hit a certain standard hard, but it doesn't sink in.

Having a data chat with your teacher shows her where more instruction is needed. By having the conversation and looking at data with the teacher instead of by yourself, you are getting the full picture. Many times, we are not in the classroom. Therefore, we don't know what the teacher has and has not done.

Data chats help create a clear pathway to a healthier teacher–coach relationship and a solid goal for the year.

Preparing for a Data Chat

Now that you know some of the benefits of data chats, what is the best way to go about having a data chat with your teachers? I have found keeping your relationship with teachers healthy to be effective, and therefore I always give teachers a heads-up about our data chats. When you plan to have a data chat with a teacher, make sure you do the following:

- Are honest about the reason for the meeting.
- Prepare teachers by having them assess certain "below" and "above" standards prior to the meeting.
- Give teachers time to round up some resources they have used or plan on using that you can look at together.
- Ensure that you have enough time to go through the data and have a good conversation.
- Have your data ready when you begin the meeting.

Allowing teachers to be prepared and being prepared yourself sets you up for success.

How to have a Data Chat

Once everyone is organized, make sure you come into the room and start with something positive. Look at a piece of data together that worked well. If you have data that improved because of something you and the teacher implemented together, that's even better to start with. Take some time to celebrate, and then get into the nitty gritty of it all, but don't go too far into the hole.

While it is important to talk about standards that need work, you may want to focus on one or two at a time. It might be good practice to show teachers the data beforehand and let them choose which standards they want to focus on first.

Regardless of how you decide which standards to focus on, make sure you don't have a million of them. Everyone knows you cannot do a thousand things at once and do them well. Piling on all the "below" standards right away can make teachers feel overwhelmed and thus they might not be as receptive to your resources or ideas.

After you discuss the standards that need work, end the meeting with a goal and a game plan. Having a goal and a plan helps keep you and the teacher accountable, and you can both leave the meeting feeling like you got something out of the data, which makes future data chats easier.

After Data Chats

I'm sure you are starting to see how great data chats can be, but to put a little icing on the cake, here are some specific benefits that can come from having a data chat with your teachers.

There are so many benefits to data chats. Not only do you walk away with a solid plan, but also you have a way to measure success with the data to truly show the students' growth in the end. So, if you haven't taken data into the classroom, pull it out, and have a conversation with your teachers about the data coming out of their classrooms. It will be worth it in the end.

- You have an obvious concept to observe.
- The teacher has a definite goal.
- Reflections become centered around a standard.
- Goals become more meaningful.
- Growth is easily shown.

While the words "professional development" might cause a few eyes to roll, PD time is a fantastic opportunity for you to use data you have collected in classrooms.

How can you use data to guide professional development? I'm glad you asked. Follow the steps below to make professional development meaningful.

Before the professional development meeting

Step 1: Gather your data

This is the legwork you need to do to be prepared for the professional development session. To be prepared, put the data you want teachers to look at together and divide it into like-mind categories. For example, you might have behavior data, reading data, math data, and so on.

You don't want to overwhelm teachers with a huge packet of papers. Dividing up the data will help make it more manageable and less cumbersome.

You can gather data from the formal and informal observations you have done throughout the year. A good practice is to review your observation notes to determine what you need to focus on and get the data together for those categories.

Step 2: Form teams

After you've collected data, you want to form teams examine the data for you. A good way to form your teams is by looking at the data categories and putting teachers who are impacted by that data into the related group.

If you are looking at middle and high school teachers, you may want to put your English teachers in the reading category and your math teachers in the math category. "Other" teachers can be divided up equally or put into "miscellaneous" categories.

If you are looking at elementary teachers, you should put them in the categories where they need the most help. For example, if a second grade teacher is great at teaching math but struggles with reading strategies, putting him in the reading data group would be appropriate.

Step 3: Set a purpose

The final piece of prep work you need to do is set a purpose for teachers as a whole or for each category. Your choice will depend on your overall goal. You should set an overall goal for the professional development session and share that with the teachers before you begin.

For example, a purpose could be to

- understand how we have improved;
- understand where we need to improve;
- create a goal to be better; and
- create resources for success.

You may have a few "purposes" or overall goals for the professional development session, and if so, that's great!

During the professional development meeting

Step 4: Beginning your professional development

You want to be positive when starting a professional development session. Talk about the good things you have seen in classrooms and what you look forward to doing either the next year or the second half of the year.

Next, tell the group what your plan is for the day and make sure it is displayed. Within your plan, you should make sure you have a scheduled break. Adding times to your plan can be helpful for keeping everyone on track.

Finally, have a "work plan" or a "task tracker" for teachers. You can have them fill out a form while they talk or just display what they need to accomplish in the amount of time they are given.

Step 5: Discussing the data

Once you explain what teachers are going to be doing and put them into their groups, they should start talking about the data. Walk around the room. When teachers are in their groups, they should start at the beginning: looking at the data and interpreting it.

As you walk around the room, you should hear teachers discussing trends they are noticing in the data that are both positive and negative.

Step 6: Group share

Once teachers have been given an adequate amount of time to look at the data, ask them to share what they found.

During this time, you or a designated person should record the positive and negative factors the teachers observed in the data. Display the notes being taken in some way, whether on a large piece of paper or projected on a big screen.

Sharing the observations about the data is important because teachers should be aware of the whole picture not just a little piece of the puzzle.

<u>Step 7: Setting goals</u>

Once you have discussed the data as a whole group, teachers should be setting goals. There are two ways to set goals.

> <u>Option 1:</u> Have teachers return to their groups and set goals for the areas they looked at in the data. After the teachers have time to decide on a goal, have them share the goal with the group and have the goal recorded as well.
> <u>Option 2:</u> Have all the teachers join together and come up with a goal for each category. Record those goals as well.

The option you choose to use will depend heavily on the size of your school as well as the teachers' personalities.

<u>Step 8: Finding resources</u>

This is an optional step, but if you need to fill in a little more time, it is a productive use of that time. Once you set goals, you can have teachers return to their groups. Each group can create a task force and find resources that will help achieve the goals they specified in Step 7.

While professional development can be something of a "bore" when it is not used properly, using data to guide your professional development can help make the day meaningful for everyone involved.

Coaching Thought

Utilizing data as an instructional coach can be empowering for teachers, coaches, and the administration. I have learned time and time again that collecting data gets people to listen and is vital to your success as an instructional coach and the success of teachers. Just promising people that they will grow in their teaching and classroom management skills can be vague, and it may be hard to help them see how much they are improving. Collecting and tracking data allows for reflection; hosting data chats allows for correction and planning; and creating professional development around what teachers' need, rather than the trends in education, allows for meaningful and purposeful learning. Together, you will see great changes in student achievement.

What are your key takeaways from utilizing data, and what do you plan to do first?

_____

_____

_____

_____

_____

_____

_____

_____

_____

_____

_____

_____

_____

_____

How do I find a starting point with a teacher and develop a coaching plan?

If you have been appointed to work with a teacher and are new to coaching or are new to the school and haven't received much direction, knowing where to begin can be overwhelming. I have worked with administrators who had a vision for coaching that wasn't what coaching was all about. As a result, the administrative direction was misguided in terms of the issues that needed to be addressed. You may be pointed in the direction of a handful of teachers who have weaker data than their teammates. Finding out where the root of the problem lies is critical. Do not assume that weak data means the teacher just needs help with teaching the content. Poor content knowledge or holding misconceptions about different standards can certainly result in poor data. But let's not forget all the other things that can cause a group of students to fail to meet their potential. Poor classroom management, lack of differentiation, poor engagement, and teacher bias against a group of students are just a few issues that can result in low student achievement.

How do you know where to begin? This question is easier to answer than you might think. You were an excellent teacher, right? How did you know where to begin in your classroom? You most likely started the year with routines and procedures and then spent some time building your classroom community. Likewise, spend time with teachers who may need coaching, keep an eye out for hallmark lessons, and check in with how they are going. The theme of my first meeting with teachers is "cupcakes with coach," which helps me get to know the teachers and also enables me to see exactly how the teachers perceive coaching and their own needs.

While completing your greeting rounds, if you come across a teacher who is struggling with management or who doesn't appear to be prioritizing teaching tasks, you may have found the true root of the problem. Work with such teachers and set them up for success as you both progress through the year.

If a teacher avoids teaching small groups and prefers that everyone do the same work the same way, you will need to home in on differentiation and reteaching small group skills to help that teacher improve. Every classroom will have its own struggles, but you need to take the time to uncover those problems. Furthermore, you can take the best practices you used as a teacher and transfer those to your work as a coach.

After you complete several observations and are familiar with the problems in the classrooms, it is time to develop coaching plans. A coaching plan outlines how you will work with a teacher and provides a roadmap to improving instruction. There is no one-size-fits-all coaching plan. Each teacher's needs will be different, and the way you approach their needs will be different. I like to compare this to the classroom strategy called differentiation. When you teach a group of students, you usually assess their needs through a pre-assessment process. You then create lesson plans based on the information from the pre-assessments. You can do the same when you begin coaching teachers.

Let's look at how you can create a plan of action for each of your teachers. As I said, each teacher will require a different type of coaching. Some will need help in becoming more focused on the delivery of content and in managing strategies. Some will need help creating powerful lessons. Some will need help with resources. As the coach, it is your job to identify the type of coaching a teacher needs and to provide the teacher with that particular support.

When developing a coaching plan, it is important that you utilize the coaching cycle. The coaching cycle will help you deliver the actions in the plan. But let's look at the steps to creating the actual plan.

Step 1: Assess the needs of the teacher. You want to conduct a baseline observation. A baseline observation is when you visit and observe a teacher in a classroom for approximately 30 to 40 minutes. You write a script of everything you see and focus on (1) learning targets, (2) learning environments, (3) instructional execution, (4) assessment/checks for understanding, and (5) student academic behavior.

Step 2: Review the data. You want to look at the area in which your teacher needs the most work. These needs usually fall under three categories: (1) classroom management and culture, (2) content planning and execution, and (3) development of rigorous curriculum and assessing and identifying resources.

Step 3: Tier teachers and identify possible supports. When I support teachers, I place them in tiers. I use the three-tier pyramid method, the RTI pyramid that we all know and love. I place teachers in each tier based on the following:

Tier 1 Teachers

> have taught three+ years;
> do not need classroom management/procedures/routine support;
> need support in building rigor in lessons;
> reflect on current practices being used;
> modify teaching strategies;
> need little support to complete day-to-day functions; and
> receive and apply feedback in a positive way.

> Possible support:
> Monthly/bi-monthly classroom observations
> Semester or quarter coaching cycle goals
> Gradual release of responsibility approach
> Student-focused coaching cycle (Diane Sweeney)
> Virtual resources for support
> Weekly email check-ins

Tier 2 Teachers

> have taught two to five years;
> need support in classroom management and lessons;
> receive and apply feedback in a positive way;
> modify teaching strategies; and
> need some support to complete day-to-day functions.

> Possible support:
> Bi-weekly classroom observations
> Three or four school weeks or 15- to 20-day coaching cycle goals
> Gradual release of responsibility approach
> Teacher-centered coaching (Diane Sweeney)
> Virtual resources for support

Tier 3 Teachers

> have taught 0 to 1 years;
> can be a teacher with multiple years;
> need support in classroom management and lesson development;
> receive and apply feedback in a positive way;
> need support in modifying teaching strategies; and
> need lots of support to complete day-to-day functions.

> Possible support:
> Weekly classroom observations
> Two-school-week coaching cycle goal or 10-day coaching cycle goal
> Gradual release of responsibility approach
> Only one or two issues at a time
> Virtual resources for support
> Weekly face-to-face and email check-ins

I use the above as a guide for mapping out what my year may look like. All teachers may not fit into these categories perfectly, but in my experience, it is a pretty good guide.

Step 4: Meet with your teacher and write the plan. You have completed Steps 1–3 and have some idea of where your teachers need help and what type of support you will need to provide, and now you are ready to meet with your teachers.

You want to base your coaching plan on your observations, the tier you place teachers in, and the goals you have set together. (BTW: Teachers don't know that you tier them; it is for tracking and support purposes only. It helps you know how many teachers you will need to meet with weekly versus bi-weekly versus monthly.)

Say that the big goal is that at least 80% of students will score "Proficient" on the state math exam at the end of the year, but step one of that goal is that 80% of students will pass the next unit test. Let's also say that one teacher is a first-year teacher who recognizes that she doesn't know the content well yet, and her confidence is a little low. You can approach this situation with some modeling at the beginning (if the teacher is comfortable with it). You can model a whole group math lesson or a small group lesson, help plan the centers, differentiate the work, and so on. You can then gradually release responsibility either after a few days of co-teaching or after observation with feedback on the same day. You want to be really hands-on with this teacher. She set a big goal, recognized that she did not have all of the tools she needed, and was open to as much help as you can provide. This teacher will be placed in tier 3, and she will definitely need weekly support.

If, instead, a teacher has taught the same content for ten years, sets the same goal as above, and is fairly confident she will meet it, you will want to approach things differently. This teacher is likely a tier 1 teacher, so you can consider testing data with her and encourage her to challenge herself a little more. If she does more meaningful, differentiated center work on top of her small group instruction, can her students become 20% more proficient? Can she push herself so that 90% of her students are at grade level by the end of the year? This may mean that you will spend time studying Bloom's Taxonomy with her and will show her ways to add layers of questioning to the same assignment. You may not observe this teacher during the current cycle. You may simply help to guide the planning, and check back in to analyze the data. If the need for observation comes up, because the data is stagnant, then you will cross that bridge at the appropriate time. Again, when mapping out a coaching plan, it is important to approach teachers according to their needs.

The coaching plan focuses on how you will coach teachers for the year. It helps you think about the intensity of the support you will provide teachers.

Here are a few things you can include in your coaching plan:

Teacher's name
Grade she teachers
Years of experience
Teacher's yearly professional goal correlated to the school-wide goal
How the goal will be measured
Benchmark goals
Teacher's yearly personal improvement goal
Teacher's learning style

Coaching Thought

Change and improvement will happen only if you support the process. Creating a coaching plan for each teacher allows you to develop a strategic map for achieving the goal. Within the coaching plan, identifying support for each teacher allows you to be as efficient as possible. You are only one coach with multiple people to support, and in order to be the best coach you can be, you must be organized and have a mapped-out route to success. You will come upon many bumps in the road, but having a mapped-out plan is half the battle.

Write what you want to include in your coaching plan for teachers. If you already know your teachers, you can start to tier each teacher. If you don't already know them, think about how you will want to support them. Complete a "brain dump" based on the suggestions in this part and your own classroom experiences.

_____
_____
_____
_____
_____
_____
_____
_____
_____
_____
_____
_____
_____
_____
_____
_____
_____

Part V

PLCs, Team Planning and Professional Development

"Creating a collaborative culture is the single most important factor in school improvement for those seeking to enhance the effectiveness of teaching and learning."

-R. Dufour & B. Dufour

How do I lead a PLC?

First, a note: Use of the acronym PLC is widespread, and it is defined in different ways. In the context of this book, PLC stands for Professional Learning Community, based on the book from Rick DuFour.

I have learned that the key to leading a successful PLC is *not* to lead it. A PLC takes teacher ownership, and if you present yourself as the leader, the teachers will rely on you to keep the conversation going and will look to you to decide what to discuss next. Thus, if you cannot be present at a PLC meeting, the show will not go on.

In the beginning of the school year, teachers will look to you for guidance in implementing the PLC model. You will guide them in creating and establishing norms, in looking for ways to document the meeting, and in looking at data and creating assessments and ways to implement strategies. Although, as the instructional coach, you should be a part of those meetings, it is not your responsibility to lead them. You are the support in those meetings, asking probing questions to get the team to think through their issues and problems and come up with answers that will help them become successful as a team.

I recently worked with a coach who attempted to launch very data-driven PLCs in her building. The goals of creating the PLCs were to have each team collect and share data from their classrooms and to be keenly aware of how each student in their building was performing on each standard. The building's coaches led the teams through setting goals and norms and determining their core values. They made spreadsheets in Google and shared them with team members to input pretest and post-test data. We created "minutes" forms to log discussion notes from each meeting.

They also attended each grade level's planning once or twice a week to lead the PLC discussion and keep teachers on track. The woman I coached spoke of this approach as being great . . . until it wasn't. The building's coaches also served as interventionists, and one grade level's planning time might be one or two other grade level's RTI time.

The coaches had to follow coaching cycles and had lessons to model while some teachers might be in a PLC session. Even with two leaders in the building, scheduling was too much for them to perform their job. The coaches found that when they were unable to be present, the teachers did not know how to maintain the routine of the PLC. As the rigor of the year got heavier, the coaches' ability to keep up with the PLCs dwindled, and so did the teachers' interest in learning how to do it themselves.

When the woman I was coaching and I discussed the situation, she noted that the coaches did a poor job of gradually releasing responsibility. In such situations, my recommendation is to start by helping the teachers lead it. If there are team leaders, they can facilitate discussions, or maybe each person can play rotating roles (timekeeper, note taker, discussion leader, etc.). However, you decide to do it, keep the teachers at the center of the process. Do not make yourself the leader. PLCs should be focused, honest, data-driven discussions, and teachers need to know how to do that with or without you present.

Coaching Thought

Deciding on the type of PLC and understanding your principal's vision for the PLC is crucial for your planning. I have been in buildings where the PLCs were just professional development time, and we didn't dig into data until our cycle data meetings. So, in the PLCs I was responsible for providing all of the teaching. I have also been in buildings where the teams were responsible for leading the PLC meetings, and I was the support in the meeting, but didn't drive the meeting.

Ask the question, "Which type of PLC will my building implement?" And go from there. Take on the role of leading or training and support. Document which type of PLC, and think about your role and how best to support it.

_____

_____

_____

_____

_____

_____

_____

_____

_____

_____

_____

_____

_____

_____

_____

How do I use video for a PLC?

Video can be intimidating for some teachers, but I am a strong believer in its effectiveness as a teaching tool. You can film PLC sessions as a way to replace taking notes and record the minutes from sessions. That way, you always have a record of what was discussed. You can use video to record an example of a strong PLC meeting and share the video with members of other grade level teams who may not be strong collaborators.

Video can also be used to refine a team's discussion. If they play back their own PLC sessions, they may notice times when they didn't make decisions based on data, or times they got sidetracked on one topic too long, or times they left a conversation about a student unresolved. It's hard in the moment to monitor a conversation among several different teachers, but seeing the conversation on video can show a grade level team where they can tighten up their routines and where they are doing well.

Video can also be used to show a teaching strategy that a team is considering implementing. The team can watch the video and discuss how the strategy is being implemented and how they as a team will implement the strategy.

If one of the teachers implements the strategy and gets awesome results, you as the coach can videotape the teacher in action and then show the video at a PLC session and have the team discuss the video. Teachers on the team will be able to stop the video and ask questions or perhaps pick up on new ways they can implement the strategy.

Coaching Thought

Video is a great reflection tool. But careful about videotaping teachers. Some unions and districts prohibit the use of videotapes in school buildings. You are free to use videos found on the Internet, I am sure.

Check on the rules regarding the use of videos in your district. Do you need to have forms and agreements signed before you can utilize video in a PLC?

_____

_____

_____

_____

_____

_____

_____

_____

_____

_____

_____

_____

_____

_____

_____

_____

How do I set the mood for collaboration within a team?

Much of the focus of this book thus far has been on how you have the responsibility as a coach to build relationships with teachers, but a large part of leading or being a part of an effective collaborative planning meeting or PLC is making sure teachers have a good relationship with each other.

Norms and team values are important parts of a productive, successful planning meeting and PLC. Earlier I noted that your role as a coach is to be a support during PLCs. You will, of course, lead the first meeting, but you will assign teachers the task of coming up with five to ten team norms, as well as their core values as a team. Doing so helps them unite as teachers and gives them the chance to voice their opinions about their own values. Taking the time to do this lets all the teachers know that their ideas are valued and that these planning meetings are a safe space to voice opinions. This approach can lay the foundation for a great year.

Coaching Thought

At the beginning of each meeting, you can "set the mood" for team collaboration by having the teachers revisit the norms they set and read their core value(s) aloud. This reminds everyone of why they are there, not to serve their own agenda but to serve their students. Doing so can ensure that side-table conversations don't happen and that extra work is put away, allowing everyone to focus as they prepare to share ideas.

Do you have a planning sheet for teachers to develop norms? Or sample norms? If not, check out the next question and write a few.

_____
_____
_____
_____
_____
_____
_____
_____
_____
_____
_____
_____
_____
_____
_____

What are some sample meeting norms for teams?

As I mentioned in the preceding section, stating norms at the beginning of a meeting can help teachers refrain from griping or venting about their students and focus on planning and strategizing about ways to help their students. The list of norms below may evoke thoughts about a list of your own (you may want to share this list with teachers).

- All team members will arrive and be ready to begin meeting no later than five minutes after planning time begins.
- All team members will arrive with materials they need.
- Cell phones will be silenced and out of view during PLC/planning.
- Everyone will have the chance to voice their opinions and share their ideas.
- All team members have the right to agree or disagree with other team members without judgement.
- Any discussions about student data will be kept professional and will not leave the room.
- All suggestions, ideas, and opinions shared will be student-centered and data-driven.

Coaching Thought

Norms are very important for hosting effective meetings with teams of teachers. Creating the norms together allows the team members to build trust with one another and to all feel valued.

Create norms you
will introduce to
your teams.

_____

_____

_____

_____

_____

_____

_____

_____

_____

_____

_____

_____

_____

_____

_____

_____

_____

How do I plan a book study with teachers?

A book study can be a highly effective method of providing professional development to your staff. You can stand on the shoulders of published experts to present topics your teachers need to investigate further and then help them process the information. Book studies are hands-down one of my favorite ways to provide professional development, but it can be difficult to highlight every important point an author makes in a book. We don't have limitless time to discuss a great book with our staff, so below are ways that I've approached such studies.

<u>Choose a book</u> that you have already read and feel strongly about, if you can. There are occasions when your administration or district personnel may have chosen a book they want everyone to study, and you are the elected person to lead the study. If that's the case, read the book before you do any planning. However, if you have free reign and based on your walkthroughs and discussions with teachers, narrow your choices to books on topics your staff needs exposure to. If you've already read books and can vouch for their worthiness, great! If you haven't, take the time to read one, or at least *most* of one. A book study is really hard to lead if you're reading alongside your teachers. You can try it, but consider yourself warned.

It is important to get teachers' buy-in for a book study. If you have the option of multiple books, allow the staff to vote on the book they want to read. Doing so can avoid having them see the activity as just "another thing to do," but as a way to improve their craft as an educator.

<u>Map the meetings</u> around two to four different chunks of a book. It may be that parts of the staff meetings are dedicated to discussions on the entire book, or you could offer book study meetings as after-school professional development credit. Regardless, figure out how many meetings you will hold, and divide the book up appropriately. The first meeting could focus on Chapters 1 through 4, and so on.

Before the teachers begin reading a section, <u>send them discussion questions</u> to consider. When I prepare my questions, I include lines where they can record notes as they read, but that's totally optional. However, doing so helps direct teachers' attention to the parts of the book you deem most important, and it will keep you from being met with silence when you hold the book discussion. Teachers will have thought through their responses already and will be more likely to share them with the group. This also holds teachers accountable. Next school year, I am planning to host my book study online, where I will post discussion questions in an online classroom; teachers, in turn, will submit their responses there as well as respond to others' responses.

<u>Determine action steps and reflection tasks for teachers</u> for each section. I recommend only one or two points that you want teachers to take from the book and try in their classrooms. Give them a reflection task as "homework, and let them know that you want to hear how things went the next time you come together. Be sure to space these meetings so teachers have enough time to read and consider their answers to your discussion questions and to try the action step from the previous meeting. In my school, next year we will videotape one teacher volunteer implementing a strategy from the book. The video will be played at one of the book study meetings and discussion among the teachers will follow.

Book studies typically can't be done in a week or two. I love when a school has a book that is centered around its vision, and the teachers dive deep into the book over the course of an entire semester, or even a year. If you don't have that kind of time, you can simplify and shorten these steps, in which case, my advice is to revisit the book's principles throughout the year as a reminder.

Coaching Thought

For a book study to be effective, you must ensure that it is interactive and purposeful. The book must align with what is needed and happening in the classroom. Otherwise, it's a waste of time.

Can you host a book study the upcoming school year? If so, consider your school's vision and goals and try to find a book that matches them, and check whether the budget will allow you to purchase a book for each teacher. Lastly, how will you hold teachers accountable for participating?

_____

_____

_____

_____

_____

_____

_____

_____

_____

_____

_____

_____

_____

_____

_____

_____

How can I gather ideas for professional development to offer to staff?

Usually, the instructional coach is responsible for presenting professional development to the staff. There is no shortage of ideas, but you want to be sure to offer training on topics that are relevant and interesting to the teachers. I have gathered input and data in different ways to create professional development topics that are relevant and purposeful.

Send a survey to the staff. You can email an open-ended questionnaire near the beginning of the year, asking teachers what professional development topics they would like to focus on. Chances are that your district or state has been pushing teachers to do certain things, but the teachers feel ill-equipped to do so. You will likely notice themes.

Think about the expertise teachers need to fulfill the school's vision. Your principal may have set a goal for the school to achieve a certain score on the state's end of year math exam, or your district may want 80 percent of students to pass the state writing test. There is probably an initiative in your area around which you could plan a whole set of professional development sessions.

Complete walkthroughs and discuss them with the administration. By the third week of school, everyone is in their groove of teaching. I set aside two days to complete walkthroughs in the classrooms. I do about three or four in each class over the two-day period during two different times of the day. I write notes about what I see, but not specific to particular teachers. I work with the administration team as well so that I can get multiple perspectives. We meet and discuss trends we see happening in the building and identify a few topics based on those trends.

Coaching Thought

Coming up with ideas for professional development is a pretty easy task. Education is a revolving door of the latest ideas and strategies and how to carry them out. Don't just jump on the latest bandwagon; instead, give teachers what they need to be successful in the classroom.

Consider the survey I mentioned. What are some questions you may need to ask your teachers? Jot them down.

_____
_____
_____
_____
_____
_____
_____
_____
_____
_____
_____
_____
_____

How do I develop a professional development calendar?

In many districts, instructional coaches are the primary person responsible for delivering professional development at the building level. There are two ways to look at developing a professional development calendar, and they are based on what time of day you will deliver the sessions: during school hours or after school hours. This makes a big difference when looking at developing a calendar because so much must be considered.

Here are a few questions to ask before you start:

- What time of day will I be presenting? During the regular school hours? During teachers' planning times? During regular grade level or content-specific meetings?
- Is this professional development mandatory for teachers to attend or is it completely voluntary?
- Will all of my teachers be attending?

Once you get some clarity, you will know how to proceed.

In my current role as a building coach, I am required to deliver biweekly professional development sessions to all classroom teachers. Since I know I will deliver biweekly, I map out my topics at the beginning of the school year based on the school's initiatives. For instance, if the school is working on developing teachers in the area of rigor, then I backward design that topic. I describe what I want the teachers to be able to do when the training is over and what evidence I will need to show that a teacher has implemented the strategy and is working through the reflection or delivery of the strategy. Once I know what I want to see, I then start to plan how to introduce that strategy and give titles to each session. I consider roadblocks that might occur and try to make sure that there are sessions built in for reflection and implementation struggles. I also include work sessions with teachers on specific topics.

I follow this model with all initiatives that need to be introduced and supported. Then I strategically place those on the calendar according to their importance along with a good time to start a series of professional development sessions. (You don't want to start new sessions during state testing; teachers will not be engaged.)

Then I look at my remaining sessions. I plan sessions to review previous topics and leave space for sessions based on walkthrough data. I write or enter those into my calendar.

After my calendar is developed, I share it with my administrators. Everyone on the team must understand that the calendar I create at the beginning of the year is a working document, meaning it can change at any time. There will be times when you will need to push a session back, add a session on a different topic, and so forth. Think of this as your curriculum map. Sometimes in the classroom, we have to get off the map to ensure that students master a foundational skill before we can move on. The same happens when developing a professional development calendar.

I don't usually share my yearlong, biweekly topic calendar with teachers because, as I mentioned, topics can change. I send a weekly newsletter to teachers that includes the topic of the session during that week. The only exception is when I'm doing an ongoing series of sessions about a specific strategy and I need teachers to implement it and return with evidence and feedback. That's usually when they are aware of the topics ahead of time.

When I was a district coach, I delivered professional development after school to teachers who worked in specific schools. My method of development for the calendar and plan was the same except that I had another thing to consider, the budget. Every school district is different when it comes to professional development outside of work hours or after school. I've worked with coaches whose districts put a number of required outside professional development hours in the teaching contracts. Some districts pay a certain hourly rate for teachers to attend the sessions, and some districts offer professional development certification hours. This rule applies to any school, public, private, charter, or township. You must understand and consider this requirement before you plan professional development outside contract hours.

In my role as a district coach, the teachers I coached were paid a specific hourly rate to attend the sessions once a month. It was mandatory that they attended, so I could hold them accountable for what was being taught when I went to buildings and wanted to see the implementation.

For the sessions, each month I chose topics that were on a continuum, and I knew that I had enough sessions to front-load information and follow up with actionable support during implementation. With all that in mind, I assigned a topic to each professional development session and shared that information with my director. If you are a building coach but provide professional development outside of work hours, you can use this method to plan your sessions and share the information with your administrators.

This is a lot of information, and you may not have made such plans before or been as thoughtful in your planning. But that's okay. When starting out, you don't necessarily need to have a detailed description for each session right away. Just plug the topics into a calendar template on paper, or on something like Google Calendar (if your school has embraced Google as a learning tool), or in your instructional coaching planner (check out Simply Coaching + Teaching website). Get a start and keep developing and moving. Remember that this is a working document and can be changed based on feedback.

Coaching Thought

Offering professional development to teachers is one of the highlights of being an instructional coach. Making sure the professional development topics are relevant, purposeful, and actionable is key.

Decide on a few topics you will present. Map out an outline of the sessions.

_____

_____

_____

_____

_____

_____

_____

_____

_____

_____

_____

_____

_____

_____

What are the components of an effective professional development session?

Transitioning from teaching students to teaching adults can be a scary process. Adults are a little harder to handle because you expect them to have the desire to learn, and sometimes a teacher who is in a classroom all day can be a little reluctant to learn. Nevertheless, teaching students is very similar to teaching adults. Not that the same methods will work for both, but the process is very similar. For the past seven years, I have worked with teachers and created professional development sessions to help teachers and instructional coaches to improve professionally. My process resembles the one I used when developing lesson plans for students.

Here are the nonnegotiable components to include and remember when developing an effective professional development session:

Make the topic relevant to your audience. When teachers attend a professional development session, they want to know how the topic will connect with their everyday role as teachers. You want to start your session with the WHY. That sets the tone for everything. You must use a hook and grab the teachers' attention immediately. If you don't get them involved and make it seem relevant immediately, they will tune out and you will lose them. A hook could be a prompting question, a quick video clip, or a discovery activity, but get them to thinking. Make sure they spend only three to five minutes on this activity. Making the activity too long will allow them to have sidebar conversations and lose focus. As soon as you can, connect the hook with what they will learn and connect that to how it will help them become better teachers and increase student achievement. Once you have them on your team, you can proceed with your teaching

<u>Throw the lecture out the door.</u> When you observe a teacher in a classroom, you are watching to see whether he engages students in the learning process. Standing in front of a group of teachers, clicking through a PowerPoint presentation and just talking is, well . . . boring. And the teachers will not be engaged in the materials. Yes, there will be a time during your session when you will directly instruct teachers and provide them with background information and other essential facts related to the topic. However, you can do so in ways that will keep the teachers involved. When imparting information, I utilize probing questions. I also use the technique of storytelling. I use humor as well. While I am talking, I try to tell stories that are relevant to my audience and give them examples of things that have happened to me in the classroom. Just remember, have a conversation with your audience. Don't talk at them.

<u>Build background knowledge.</u> The worst thing in the world is to present a professional development session to teachers who do not know what you are talking about. Sometimes, you must provide a bit of background information on topics you are presenting, especially when the strategy or curriculum is new. Discuss briefly the source of the information or relate the strategy to a previous strategy that teachers know and understand. Providing that information will give teachers a point of reference and help them connect the dots.

<u>Provide guided time during which teachers learn from each other by incorporating discovery and highly engaging activities and opportunities.</u> "Tell me and I forget. Teach me and I remember. Involve me and I learn." This quotation attributed by some to Benjamin Franklin says it all. When you are teaching people, whether adults or children, you must allow them to grapple through a process, practice it, and develop it in order to fully understand it —and then, at some point, apply it. When I am presenting, I always allow group time and individual time for teachers to implement whatever I am presenting. If I am teaching them how to develop assessment questions, I divide them into groups and give them sample assessment questions. Based on the

information I presented, the teachers conduct a sort activity. They may have a checklist of questions to ask each other as they are sorting, which will spark conversations about the information I presented and will also ensure that they are using that information. If they do not understand the content, I am there to give immediate feedback and provide clarity. They can also get clarity from one another because they are working in groups. If I am presenting on a strategy of some sort, I will use that strategy in my presentation so that the teachers can experience it.

Check for understanding. When you are teaching a classroom full of students, you have to stop and read the room, ask questions, check body language, observe conversations, and say, "If you are with me, raise your hand." You must do the same when presenting to adults. You need to ensure that your audience is with you. Checking for understanding lets you know whether teachers are on the same page you are, and if not, you can switch quickly and explain the concept in a different format or with a different example.

Keep it moving! I use timers when presenting. Why? Because you can easily get caught up on one thing and lose your audience. When I plan out a forty-five minute session, it may look like this:

- 5 minute introductions (flexible if you present to the same group; use for quick commitment updates)
- 5 minute hook (relevance)
- 15 minute direct instruction (background information, new concept, storytelling)
- 7 minute group activity (guided application)
- 7 minute share out and discussion
- 6 minute wrap up/next steps

Looking at this outline, you can see that there is not much time for professional development and really no wiggle room. So to ensure that I present all the information, provide clarification, and follow up with teachers, I need to stay the course; and timers work perfectly for that. Timers also give a sense of urgency and allow for little down time, which prevents sidebar conversations.

Always discuss next steps and the follow-up. If teachers are aware that you will follow up on this information, they will take it seriously. How many times have you attended a professional development session and it was great information and very helpful and gave you a boost, but when you implemented it, it failed. You had no one to help you troubleshoot what went wrong, and even worse, no one ever mentioned it again. So the training and strategy that was so awesome and great in theory failed you and went by the wayside. Letting teachers know that you will be meeting with them to discuss how the implementation went, planning with them, observing them, or letting them know what professional development topics will be next will help them understand the importance of the information. At the end of my sessions, I have teachers sign a commitment. "Make a commitment to implement xyz by xyz. . . ." I provide a big Post-it note and let them write exactly what they will implement and then sign the note. We always start our next session with a discuss and debrief period focused on how the commitment went. I also have documentation of who is doing what, and when we have our one-on-one meetings, I am able to prepare resources or have specific questions ready to discuss.

Coaching Thought

Professional development is only as effective as the presentation, and the ability to grab the audience and get them involved in their learning is a big part of the process. So plan on using engaging activities and following the preceding advice.

Choose two areas that you want to work on and brainstorm ways that you can improve them.

_____
_____
_____
_____
_____
_____
_____
_____
_____
_____
_____
_____
_____
_____
_____
_____

Part VI

Building Relationships, Trust with Teachers, and Dealing with Conflict

"No significant learning can occur without a significant relationship"

- Dr. James Comer

How can I build relationships with adults?

Building relationships with adults is not all that different from building relationships with students in a classroom. Take a second to reflect on how you, as a teacher, approached the first week of school. You probably wanted to make students feel comfortable in your room, you wanted to make your expectations clear, and you wanted to show your personality in a way that would help students connect with you.

Adults are no different. It's important to make personal connections with your teachers. Share things about yourself that will help bridge the gap between you and the teachers in your building. Don't make it all about business all of the time. A few years ago, I was supporting a building coach, and it was a big issue with some teachers in the building. The teachers were very negative, especially one teacher. She questioned everything we did and refused to be a part of the team. In one of the meetings, the teachers were working on incorporating a strategy into their lesson plans. I decided to have a one-on-one conversation with the defiant teacher. We talked and bit, and I discovered that she was a fairly new mom. Her son was about eleven months and was struggling with asthma. Both of my boys had asthma, and my oldest son was diagnosed at six months. I began to talk with her about some of the treatments that my son had and some of the things he went through. As a mom who understood what was happening to her, I was able to connect with her on a personal level, only then could we get to the lesson planning. She was really just frustrated with all the changes that were happening—and dealing with a sick baby is enough to send any mom into worryland. Her refusal wasn't about school; it was about handling everything that was being thrown at her all at once. I let her know that I understood her reactions and that they were okay. After that, she felt better, and from that point on she got right onboard.

You will not be able to connect with all your teachers in this way, but you can let your guard down and try to find a common denominator that will help you make a connection. At the same time, you want to modestly but clearly establish that you are a coach mandated to bring your professional expertise to the table. This can be done when you are leading professional development sessions, sharing information at staff meetings, emailing resources through monthly newsletters, and many other ways. To the best of your ability, build relationships with the staff in your building You want to strike a chord between being professional and being relatable. Making connections is step one; from there the relationship will build over time.

Coaching Thought

Be human and share your experiences. Letting teachers know who you are, beyond being their coach, can help them feel comfortable with you.

What strategies did you, as a teacher, use at the beginning of the school year to connect with students? Consider how you can use those same strategies to connect with your teachers.

_____

_____

_____

_____

_____

_____

_____

_____

_____

_____

_____

_____

_____

_____

_____

_____

_____

How can I work with teachers who have a fixed mindset?

I once worked in a building where staff morale was very low and teachers' interest in growth and improvement felt nonexistent. Although the occasional teacher pushed himself to be better, as a whole, each team seemed stuck in their routines. When I tried to implement the PLC cycle in the building, it crashed and burned because no one felt safe exposing their vulnerabilities in teaching. Everyone wanted to present themselves as being perfect, and if the data suggested otherwise, a myriad of excuses and defenses ran the conversation.

That's where you have to start: creating a safe space for teachers to be vulnerable. If you haven't built a trusting relationship with a teacher, and you try to have a conversation about something you want him to try, you will likely get a list of excuses about how others are standing in his way. I have heard teachers say their students are lazy, their students are too low, their parents don't care, the district sets up too many obstacles, and on and on and on. When these kinds of excuses pop up, it signals me that the teacher doesn't believe that he is good enough for whatever I am pushing him to do. He sees the low socioeconomic status of the students as a stumbling block, and a shield to hide behind. He doesn't see it as a challenge to him as a teacher or as an opportunity to serve those who need help the most. Teachers can overcome such defensive attitudes, but they need to know and trust that the people on their team have their back.

Shifting such mindsets must start at the top. The principal should instill a growth community by observing often, providing constant feedback, and hosting discussions about strengths and weaknesses. I have learned that I can attempt to do these things alone, but if the principal undermines these ideals by treating observations as a task on her to-do list, and not as a valuable opportunity for discussion, or avoids difficult conversations with teachers, then you end up feeling like you are spinning your wheels. It's important that you and your principal share the same vision for the school (see more on that topic below), because you will get so much further with fixed-mindset teachers when you are a team.

If you do not have the support of the principal, or even if you do but you are blazing the trail, I recommend that you set small, incremental goals that are easy to attain in a short period of time. Set a goal around the next unit test or a classroom management strategy that takes a small change on the teacher's part. Encourage and praise her when that goal is met. It may sound trivial, because you are working with adults, but I promise that a teacher will not turn down her favorite coffee in the morning, with a note from you saying how impressed you are with her openness to grow. Slowly but surely, you will get this teacher to open up to the idea of taking on large changes in her classroom that she initially may have dismissed as being too hard to do. It takes a little longer, but you can effect change in this teacher's classroom the same as any other, as long as you have patience and trust that small gains in growth lead to big changes over time.

Coaching Thought

Changing someone's mindset is a process. Don't expect things to change overnight. Stay the course, give praise, and keep pushing the teacher to see the positive. Don't get caught up in negative talk and always relate everything you do to improving students' learning.

On your calendar, each month set a date by which you will have completed positive feedback walkthroughs with your teachers. Think of a theme for each month. Check out the Themed Positive Feedback forms on the Simply Coaching and Teaching Shop for ideas.

_____
_____
_____
_____
_____
_____
_____
_____
_____
_____
_____
_____
_____
_____
_____
_____
_____
_____
_____
_____

What is the best way to transition from teacher to coach with my old teammates?

I have not personally experienced transiting to a coaching position in a building where I was a classroom teacher, but I have worked with several coaches who have. I asked those coaches to weigh in on their advice for you and here is what they had to say.

This advice is from Shannon H. from Dallas, Texas:

> If you have other coaches in your building, let someone else take the lead with your old team for a while. I was fortunate to be in this position: I had a co-coach, and we shared all grade-levels and subjects. We coached more on a "What am I better at" basis. She was the queen of kindergarten and first grade. She had a lot of strengths when it came to classroom management for little ones, and she knew phonics instruction and number sense like the back of her hand. I am really more of an upper elementary teacher at heart. I also am a very techy teacher. It made sense for us for the first few months to divide up the coaching duties K-2, and 3-5. I had been teaching 2nd grade there that previous year, and I was relieved that if one of my former teammates needed help, they wouldn't need to come to me.
>
> This only lasted for a while, because at the end of the day, I knew the second grade better than my co-coach, and I had a relationship to build off of with my old team. I just didn't want to overwhelm them at the beginning by seeming too pushy and trying to assert myself too soon. You have to take the time to build relationships with them in a new way: show them you are still the same old friend they've always had, but now they can approach you with questions and get feedback in a way that they wouldn't have thought to before.

This advice is from Candance Z. from Chicago, Illinois:

> If you can maintain a couple of the traditions you had with that team, do it! But don't overdo it. I still went and ate lunch with my old team at least once a week. Those girls were my best friends in the building, and that didn't change just because I was the coach. It was too sad to me to think that because I moved my stuff out of their hallway and into an office, that we couldn't be friends. However, sometimes they had team planning or they were celebrating birthdays together, or something was going on where it was clearly a "team" activity, and I would have to turn around and walk back to my office. It's important to maintain the balance of "we are still friends here and outside of the building," and "our roles are different now, and I'm not going to push in to places I am not invited." Coaching is lonely, and it's hard to not have a formal team, especially if you loved your old team. There were several people in my building in the same boat as me, and sometimes we (the gifted teacher, school psychologist, related arts teachers, etc.) would all try to eat together. That's harder to schedule, because we all have such different schedules. But, if it works out for you in your building, try to adopt a new team so you don't always feel like an island!

This advice is from John T. from Washington, DC:

> Do not take things personally. Try to keep the emotions out of your coaching relationship as much as possible. You used to teach with these people, and you may have been a team lead at one point. That may mean that the team used to use a lot of your ideas. Now that you are no longer on the team, things may shift and change. Someone new is one the team, and they may have different ideas. You may think you know this team better than anyone, and therefore you should be the one coaching them, but they may not look the same after a couple of months without you. That's ok, and change is good! Try your hardest to not have your feelings hurt if your ideas are rejected by people you consider your friends. They may not love every suggestion you make now that you are coach, which wouldn't hurt your feelings if it were a team you never worked with before. Maintain the same level of professionalism you would give any team, and do not let your emotions get the best of you.

Coaching Thought

Stepping into a new role within the same building can be hard. Think about the tips from the three coaches quoted above. Try easing into coaching with your previous team, try to maintain some of the things you guys did together, and don't take it personal if things start to change. This is a new dynamic not only for you but also for them.

Does the above situation apply to you? If so, consider the previous tips when thinking about how you, now as a coach rather than a teacher, will approach going back into your building the next school year. What will you continue doing? How will you ease into the new role? How will you support the new team member who took your spot on the team?

_____

_____

_____

_____

_____

_____

_____

_____

_____

_____

_____

_____

_____

_____

_____

How do I deal with conflict among teachers on a team?

Guiding a team of teachers through a PLC or book study can be difficult if there is unresolved tension among the members. Although it is not your job to be a mediator of conflict, if teachers are not getting along, you may not be able to carry out the duties and responsibilities specified in your job description, which can be frustrating.

I have worked with a few teams whose members disliked each other based on what I call "silly stuff." Although one team treated each another with respect in meetings, they talked about each other behind their backs and complained to the principal about each other constantly. The members of another team were rude to each other during team meetings. If one person was speaking, the others interrupted her, and they never agreed on anything. When working with that team, I had to create some norms for our meeting times. I used one of the most common strategies to address the fact that the teachers couldn't get a word in without being cut off. I used the "talking book." Everyone would be invited to share their opinions when they had the book in their hands. In this way, only the person who held the book could talk. Everyone else had to be respectful and quiet until the person with the book completely finished talking.

When you have a team with internal conflicts, it's best to create a list of norms, present the list to the team, get their feedback, and thereafter read it at the beginning of each meeting. This encourages everyone to "check their baggage" at the door and maintain a professional demeanor.

Another recommendation is to set a student-centered goal that you revisit during each meeting. Each topic you discuss with the team should be aligned with this goal. This approach will help keep emotions in check.

Teachers in conflict sometimes let their minds wander away from what is best for their students. Their language starts to become self-centered rather than student-centered. You don't need to hold an emotional pow-wow with everyone in order to clear the air: they can do that on their own time. Instead, you need to keep moving forward and send gentle, yet persistent, reminders that you are all there for the students, and that is where everyone's heads and hearts need to remain for the duration of the meeting.

Coaching Thought

Working with a team that is not focused on student achievement can be difficult. Try your best to encourage everyone to stay the course and help to make sure that student achievement is the focus by putting things in place for teachers to be reflective.

How can you help if you encounter a team that doesn't get along? Jot down any ideas that come to mind for future reference.

_____

_____

_____

_____

_____

_____

_____

_____

_____

_____

_____

_____

_____

_____

_____

_____

How do I build a relationship with my principal?

Building a relationship with your principal is essential to being an effective coach to classroom teachers. Understanding the vision for your position and being able to communicate the needs of your teachers to your principal are critical. If you are new to your building, start by having a beginning of the year meeting with the principal, where you can both discuss your values in education and what led you to being an instructional coach. This will jumpstart the conversation of your principal's vision of your role and an outline of expectations. If you are continuing at the same school, your beginning of the year meeting may be more of a recap of the previous year and a discussion on how to continue your previous work. Starting the year with this type of meeting will lay the foundation for the work that needs to be done.

Whether you are new or returning, be sure to seek clarity in your specific responsibilities, as the coaching roles in different buildings have different requirements. I've had coaches who served under several principals, and the coaches' roles varied greatly in each setting. Whereas, there are foundations like coaching cycles, presenting professional development and supporting the development of new classroom teachers, some buildings my role included being the data coach, test coordinator, and I had morning and lunch duty. The additional responsibilities varied at each building at which I coached.

If you coach teachers in multiple buildings, set a date and time to meet with each principal before the school year begins. Yes, you may need to have these meetings on your own time during the summer, but it behooves you to do so. Each principal will have different expectations, and before the craziness of the school year begins, you want to get a handle on those expectations and how you can give your best to the teachers in those buildings.

After meetings are on the list of things to do, think about how you want to approach the responsibilities that you and the principal will devise together. Be prepared to talk with your principal about how you want to work with him. This way, you will be prepared to express your concerns and desires when the two of you meet. In my meetings, I have shared that I want to take the "team" mentality, in which each month we set up a time to do walkthroughs together, Doing so will allow us to discuss what we see happening in the classroom and know that we are on the same page when I give feedback to teachers. Nothing is more frustrating to a teacher (or a coach) than when she is observed by a coach and is given feedback and then the principal observes and gives totally different feedback. In such cases, teachers will no longer take what you say seriously because the principal is the evaluator and that is the person they look to for approval. Since your role is to help teachers improve, connecting with your principal and getting his thoughts is essential. As a team, the principal should also support your work related to delivering professional development. In your principal's emails to the staff, he should definitely mention your professional development sessions and the topics; if you present a strategy at a staff meeting, the principal should follow up with why the strategy is important. If you can approach your school year as a team, two positives will happen: your staff will view what you say as being equal to the words of the principal (which will carry you far), and you and your principal will have a strong bond.

Next in your beginning of the year meeting, discuss your commitment to building trust with teachers and the confidentiality you will have with them. Your role as an instructional coach is not to be a snitch for the principal. Yes, you will discuss things you are working on and you will complete walkthroughs together, but you must hold the details of your conversations with teachers confidential. You are not supposed to observe a teacher for the principal and do a write up that will be utilized in an evaluation. Doing so is not consistent with the coaching support role.

A few years ago, I worked with an assistant principal who thought that it was my job to give her a report on things that were happening in a particular teacher's classroom. She wanted me to write my observations and send them to her. In the beginning, I observed the teacher, did the write ups, and then shared them with the assistant principal. I thought she was observing the teacher as well and that we would meet to discuss our observations and how to support the teacher. I came to find out that the assistant principal was using my observations to place the teacher on a professional improvement plan. The assistant principal never actually observed the teacher, and the plan she developed for the teacher was based entirely on my observations. I then had to coach the teacher in the areas that were based on the plan. It was a horrible experience. The trust was broken between me and the teacher. She felt betrayed and became defensive and was no longer willing to place herself in a vulnerable position and allow me to help her improve. I didn't blame her at all for feeling that way. And I never regained her trust. She moved on to another school, and I learned a valuable lesson. From that point on, I let my administrators know upfront my stand on confidentiality with teachers. Let me be clear in saying this, while I value confidentiality, if a teacher is doing something that will hurt students, student achievement, families, or staff, I will have a discussion with the teacher prior to having a discussion with the principal. Student safety is my number one obligation; everything else is second to that.

Lastly, ask for protected time in your schedule. We all can be pulled into unplanned meetings, be needed to cover a class because a sub is not available, or have to complete a task that the principal deems urgent. And as a previous assistant principal and dean, I can understand all of the above, but as a coach, I must ask that some of my weekly time be protected. When in coaching cycles, you set up follow-up meetings and times to observe the strategy being implemented by a teacher and even time to plan with teachers. Setting up those times means that you have to show up. Teachers are looking for you, and they have prepared for that time with you, and if you don't show up, they lose trust in you and faith in the process. You have to show up and be present; giving the excuse that the principal needed you or you had to do something else leaves them feeling that they are not important. What if you were a teacher and had practiced a strategy and were excited to use it and get feedback from your coach and the coach didn't show up or you received an email stating the coach had something else to do and couldn't make it? Wouldn't you be less likely to work as hard the next time and risk being let down or frustrated? So during the beginning of the year meeting, I ask for protected time. I share my calendar with my administrators weekly. I use a paper calendar, take a picture of it, and email it to them. This past year, I started to do both so that they can easily access it. (I am still a paper and pencil girl living in a technology world!) If I am called by administrators to do something and have a planned meeting with a teacher, I check for an open slot on my calendar that I can devote to the meeting with the administrator. However, if I can't meet with the administrators, they won't be offended, because I had already asked for protected time, and they know I have something scheduled that can't be postponed.

Coaching Thought

Being a coach is a fine line between classroom teacher and administrator. You are bound to get pulled in both directions. Know you are the middle man. You are the support for both roles. You will support teachers by helping them understand what needs to be done in the classroom and how to get better at that and by helping them see the administration's point of view. You will support administrators by reminding them about the struggles in the classrooms and by helping them see things from that perspective. You are what keeps things grounded. Have that beginning of the year meeting, and that lays the foundation for a successful relationship with your principal as well as a successful school year.

What specific questions do you want to ask your principal or principals at the beginning of the year meeting? Write them and design a key objective agenda for the meeting to ensure you cover everything you need to discuss. Set the appointment! Write an email right now and request the time.

_____

_____

_____

_____

_____

_____

_____

_____

_____

_____

_____

_____

_____

_____

_____

_____

What are some strategies for encouraging the administration to hold teachers accountable?

If you are in a situation where you and your administration do not see eye to eye on what needs to be happening in each classroom, or (even worse) you agree but your administration shies away from conflict and lets things slide far too often, I can tell you that great change doesn't happen overnight.

You can take certain steps to encourage growth in the staff without the backing of the principal, and there are some things you can do to nudge your principal in the direction you need her to go. But before I share those ideas, remember that your principal is the one with the vision and is the leader of the ship. Recognize that you are a support anchor, meaning you help to hold everything down, for both teachers and administrators.

As much as we would love for all our teachers to get on board and push hard for students, there will be times when teachers just will not get it or refuse to work on improving. I have worked with several teachers who were and still are that way, and I've had to ask for support from my administration. Throughout this book, I have talked about protecting teachers' confidentiality, but I've tried to make it very clear that I will seek out administrators' assistance when it comes to harming student achievement. If a teacher is not getting results, and the teacher refuses to try to get better, then it's time for the administration to get involved. Sometimes administrators can be hesitant and sometimes they just don't follow through. So I use the strategy "All Involved" (it's something I made up).

The "All Involved" strategy allows you to nudge all parties in the right direction and (hopefully) promote change in your building by inviting the principal to all meetings a particular teacher attends. I invite the principal to sit in every time I meet with the teacher or the team. It's not a surprise that the principal will be there, and it's never an "I gotcha" situation, but it is a push to get everyone on the same page.

The teacher will know that the principal is in agreement with the needed change, and the principal will see your dilemma firsthand and can speak up on your behalf. The meetings are ongoing. The principal is a part of the coaching cycle, a part of the debrief session, and in fact is totally involved. Remember when I said a principal could have issues with conflict or follow through? The "All Involved" strategy compels the principal to become involved in the process, with the result that he will likely start holding the teacher accountable for making a change.

If you and the principal don't see eye to eye about a professional development topic, use the "All Involved" strategy again, but in a different way. Set meetings with your principal or administration team and go over your presentations for the professional development sessions before delivering them to staff. Ask if they would like to add anything to your notes, and if so, incorporate those additions into the professional development sessions. Invite your principal or administrators to attend the sessions and to jump in with their own commentary. This will allow the principal to feel a part of the professional development. Doing things this way has several advantages. The principal feels as though she is a part of the development, you both now see eye to eye on the topic and its delivery, and if the principal offers her opinion during the delivery, the staff will see it as being important and will take it seriously. Whenever the principal backs you up, your words will carry more weight with the staff in the future.

Coaching Thought

Sometimes administrators need help seeing what is happening in the building and classrooms. Not all teachers will be on board. You being the middleman helps to connect the dots for the sole purpose of student achievement.

How would you use the "All Involved" strategy should you need to? Write in your own words how that might work.

_____

_____

_____

_____

_____

_____

_____

_____

_____

_____

_____

_____

_____

_____

_____

_____

_____

_____

Annenburg Institute for School Reform (2010). *Instructional coaching: Professional development strategies that improve instruction.* Providence, RI: Brown University.

Blachowicz, C., Obrochta, C., & Fogelberg, E. (2005). Literacy coaching for change. *Educational Leadership, 62*(6), 55.

Casey, K. (2006). *Literacy Coaching: The Essentials.* Portsmouth, NH: Heinemann.

Cornett, J., & Knight, J. (2009). *Coaching: Approaches and Perspectives.* Thousand Oaks, CA: Corwin Press.

Garcia, SPG., Jones, D., Holland, G., & Mundy, M-E. (2013). Instructional coaching at selected middle schools in south Texas and effects on student achievement. *Journal of Instructional Pedagogies,* 115.

Lyons, C. A., & Pinnell, G. S. (2001). *Systems for change in literacy education: A guide to professional development.* Portsmouth, NH: Heinemann.

Matsumara, L. C., Garnier, H. E., & Resnick, L. B. (2010). Implementing literacy coaching: The role of school social resources. *Educational and Evaluation and Policy Analysis, 32*(2), 249–272.

Matsumara, L. C., Sartoris, M., Bickel, D. D, & Garnier, H. E. (2009). Leadership for literacy coaching: The principal's role in launching a new coaching program. *Educational Administration Quarterly, 45*(5), 655–693.

Murawski, W. (2003). *Co-teaching in the inclusive classroom. Working together to help all your students find success.* Bellevue, WA: Institute for Educational Development.

Norton, J. (2001). A storybook breakthrough. *Journal of Staff Development, 22*(4), 22–25.

Porter, G. L., & AuCoin, A. (2012). *Strengthening inclusion, strengthening schools.* Fredericton, NB: New Brunswick Department of Education and Early Childhood Development.

Schwarz, S., & McCarthy, M. (2003). Where the rubber hits the road: An in-depth look at collaborative coaching and learning and workshop instruction in a sample of effective practice schools. In *Boston Plan for Excellence.* Boston, MA: Boston Public Schools.

https://dianesweeney.com/wp-content/uploads/2015/05/Handouts-for-General-Session.pdf

If ever there were a story of overcoming trials and tribulations, it would be entitled Nicole S. Turner. Born to two loving parents, she wasn't naive about success. Her mother, a business owner turned elementary teacher, and father, a steelworker, Nicole knew what hard work looked like and what it could get you. However, she wasn't prepared for the road ahead after graduating from high school.

Her home was comfortable, perhaps too much so, as her transition to adulthood came with quite a few hurdles. From not taking college seriously to being convinced that a degree in business was her chosen path, she made her share of what she described as wrong turns. But what one would see as bad decisions were actually a cultivation of greatness. It's a common misconception that greatness can be achieved without a few bumps in the road, and bumps were what she encountered.

Nicole didn't let anything or anyone stop her; even when her path became rugged and almost unbearable she found inspiration to keep going. She mothered two beautiful children while figuring out that business school wasn't her destined route, and shortly thereafter came her youngest. They are the source of her strength, frequently referred to as the Threes. After all, good things come in threes.

Nicole fought the urge to teach on several occasions, but you can't fight what's in you. She is a natural coach, a born leader, and after a long reflective conversation with her mother, she knew she would become a teacher.

Her journey in education was no different than her journey to it, as she encountered hurdle after hurdle. She was transferred from school to school, often as a result of a discontinued position. If her journey taught her nothing else, it taught her how to coach others. Because of her experience, she was able relate not only to teachers but also to students. Over the past ten-plus years, she's experienced primary and secondary education, she's worked in the classroom and administration, and even for the state of Indiana as a turnaround and school improvement specialist. If asked her favorite, she'd respond, instructional coach; it is in this position that she's been able to shine. She's able to personally excel while coaching others to do the same.

Nicole's story is one of ups and downs, all of which contributed to her ability to mentor others. She has dedicated her life to ensuring that her colleagues have the tools they need to be phenomenal in the classroom; their effectiveness results in the success of their students. Her dedication further fueled the creation of this book. She was not content with impacting and influencing her district alone; she wanted to empower the world. Out of that determination grew <u>Simply Instructional Coaching!</u>

Made in the USA
Monee, IL
30 June 2020